Vegetarian Slow Cooker Cookbook

Lose Weight Fast, Decrease Inflammation and Rebuild Your Body to Have a Healthy Confident Living with 101 Easy Tasty Crock-Pot Slow Cooking Recipes and 14 Days Meal Plan

By Emma Okamoto

Contents

INTRODUCTION

Do you have a thought of turning into a vegetarian? Are you interested in knowing more about the vegetarian diet? Are you looking for an easy diet plan to adopt, which will enhance your health, help you be more happier and lose more weight?

If YES, then this book is written specifically for you. You will know more about the vegetarian diet and its benefits. You will get enlightened on what you should actually eat, to live a hearty and happy life. You will learn and get proficient in vegetarian cooking by following the101 mouthwatering plant based recipes.

What will you get by following a Vegetarian Diet?
1. It fights against cancer
2. It lowers the chances of acquiring cardiovascular diseases
3. It maintains blood sugar levels
4. It controls urine pH levels
5. It is a cure for arthritis
6. It helps in weight loss
7. More and more...

You may be busy for working, busy for looking after your children and the old, busy for doing other important things. You may be not familiar with cooking. You may be lazy. You may hate cooking. You may already have a slow cooker, instant pot or high pressure cooker appliance. Congratulations! This book suits for any of the above people. All you need to do is just put all the ingredients into the slow cooker, then wait for some hours, you will finally have your delicious recipes.

If you have a Slow cooker, you will get many benefits from it:
1. Time-saving; 2. Have nutritional food; 3. All seasons appliance;
4. Energy efficient; 5. Easy to transport.

So what will you find in this book?
1. Everything about the Vegetarian Diet
2. The Health Benefits of a Vegetarian Diet
3. Why the Vegetarian Diet Enhances Quick Weight Loss
4. Foods to Eat/Avoid
5. Benefits of the Slow Cooker
6. How the Slow Cooker Works

7. The Dos and Don'ts When Using Your Slow Cooker
8. 101 Delicious and Easy Vegetarian Diet Recipes
9. A Healthy 14-Day Vegetarian Diet Meal Plan
10. More and More...

Just keep reading this book! You no need to waste any time on other similar books, just cherish this one! Now many books in the market, but it will also leads you to take more time to choose or find a good book. Just stop here! This book is your right one! You will find more good information by reading and following it!

Are you ready? The treasure is waiting for you! All you need to do is just reading it and putting it into action! Best Wishes!

Chapter 1: Vegetarian Diet

A Brief Overview of the Vegetarian Diet

The vegetarian diet has been rising in popularity as one of the health boosting diets. As a result of its amazing health benefits, people are increasingly getting interested in this plant based diet. This statement can be clearly asserted through the poll that was conducted by the American Vegetarian Research Group, where the results showed that a portion of 37 percent of Americans diet contains one vegetarian meal in a week. Also, another causal factor to the popularity of this diet is in its possession of a variety of foods, which all lead to a better healthy lifestyle, is easy and fits into any age groups, at any stage of one's life. As if that is not enough, one can afford to eat to the fullest without having any fear of getting overweight or obsessed. So if you want to be healthy in the long-run, go for a vegetarian diet.

Definition of a Vegetarian Diet

To break it down to a layman's understanding, the vegetarian diet is simply a class of food that is rich in plant foods and other healthy foods, with an insignificant amount of meat and fish present in it. Generally, a vegetarian consumes unprocessed food with less meat or no meat at all in most cases.

Vegetarianism dates back to the sixth century and its traces could be found amongst the Indians, Egyptians and during the Greek civilization because; the ethos at that time forbade the molestation of the animal, which in turn promoted the vegetarian lifestyle at that time. Thereafter, some traces of vegetarianism were found in the medieval Europe that disappeared during the introduction of Christianity. Later on, till hitherto, it has since being gaining popularity.

A vegetarian diet doesn't mean the total removal of meat completely from one's eating lifestyle, no, not at all because even some vegetarian diet contains meat, but in a moderate portion. A proper vegetarian diet must include fresh vegetables, fruits, beans, whole grains, seeds and nuts. This diet focuses on giving the body all the necessary nutrition including protein, Omega 3 fatty acids, calcium, vitamin, iron, iodine and zinc.

However, research studies shows that a vegetarian diet is highly effective in increasing one's life expectancy. In other words it is good in reducing the risk of chronic diseases that are related to body weight, digestion, heart, blood sugar levels, blood pressure levels and cancer.

In the vegetarian dieting lifestyle, there are several kinds of vegetarian groups based on the eating patterns.

1- Semi-Vegetarians: This type of vegetarian diet contains meat, fish, sea food, fruits, vegetables, legumes, beans, seeds and nuts.

2- Lacto Vegetarians: Lacto vegetarians are individuals who eat milk based products like cheese and yogurt but avoid eggs, meat and seafood.

3- Lacto-Ovo Vegetarians: Ovo means eggs and as such, the Lacto-Ovo vegetarian diet contains meat, fish, seafood, eggs and dairy products.

4- Pesco Vegetarian: The individual practicing this type of vegetarian diet eat vegetables along with eggs and fish, while avoiding other meat.

5- Vegans: Vegans are individuals who strictly follow the plant based diet. They don't take milk, eggs, dairy products, seafood or anything which comes from animals. Instead, they use a vegetarian substitute for meat and other healthy foods to get some necessary nutrients.

In other words, on decreasing or giving up protein from animal based foods, this diet ensures that a vegetarian cut out of high fatty, cholesterol, sugared and sodium foods. Not only is this good for the health, it is equally beneficial to the environment because, reduction in the intake of animal foods greatly lowers the carbon footprint.

The Health Benefits of a Vegetarian Diet

On knowing what a vegetarian diet is, the next question that often pops into our minds is always "What do I even stand to gain from this diet". Well, researchers, doctors and nutritionist have agreed that plant eaters (vegetarians) often do live a healthier life compared to others and that they do have a longer life span. How? Here are the facts.

1. It fights against cancer

The plant based diet is rich in fiber and antioxidants that offer protection to the body for almost every type of cancer. Therefore, the vegetarians have a lower chance of suffering from cancers like breast cancer, mouth, esophagus, stomach, prostate, colon and bladder cancer. In fact, cancer patients are strictly advised to follow a vegetarian diet to boost immunity. Furthermore, the fiber in it also decreases the chances of digestion complications and intestinal diseases like constipation.

2. It lowers the chances of acquiring cardiovascular diseases

Since the vegetarian diet is low in cholesterol, rich in unsaturated fats and good saturated fats, it is most certainly good for the heart. Thus, the vegetarians are at a low risk of inflammation or developing cardiovascular diseases like strokes and heart attacks. A study revealed that vegetarians have one-third the risk of suffering from heart attack compared to their meat eating peers.

3. It maintains blood sugar levels

Also being a diet low in fat, devoid of junk foods, artificial sugars and sweetened foods, the vegetarians have a lower possibility of suffering from abnormal blood sugar levels which often results in diabetes. A study released by the George Washington University School of Medicine confirmed that a vegetarian's diet plays a vital role in maintaining blood sugar levels which invariably, reduces the chances of suffering from diabetes.

4. It controls urine pH levels

Low pH level in one's urine is common to find in meat consumers, which often leads to kidney stone formation. As proven in a report released by New York University Langone Medical Center, a vegetarian ensures that the pH level of urine is maintained at a high level to avoid kidney stone development in the body.

5. It is a cure for arthritis

A vegetarian diet also provides the cure for the pain from arthritis. This probiotic-rich diet creates positive effects on people suffering from pain and joint swelling by increasing their energy levels.

6. It helps in weight loss

Last but not the least, the vegetarians are leaner and have a low percentage of fat in the body compared to meat eaters. Some data suggested that to maintain weight and fight obesity, no diet is better than the vegetarian diet.

Why the Vegetarian Diet Enhances Quick Weight Loss

One of the most known health benefits of a vegetarian diet is in its capacity of fostering weight loss and obesity. It is one of the major reasons why people are gradually drifting to this particular diet lifestyle.

A vegetarian diet promotes weight loss without concentrating on cutting down the calories intake because; by nature, it is less in calories. Many studies and reports have shown that vegetarians are often thin and do have low body mass index (BMI) compared to other individuals following various calorie-restricted diets. A vegetarian meal contains fresh fruits and veggies that are low in calories, therefore if eating in larger volumes; one doesn't have to worry about keeping a check on the calories intake. And the best part is that, the ingredients used in the food are easily satisfactory, meaning, there might always be a scenario of over-eating. However, it is essential to ensure the quantity of the meals and calories are both at equilibrium.

<u>Foods to Eat</u>

The fundamental principle in your choice of foods, when following the vegetarian diet is that it should be plant based, devoid of dietary products, fats and unhealthy fats. Then, you should endeavor to prepare your meals in such a way that it contains rich plant nutrient based foods, unprocessed foods and also ensure to get the nutrition in the right amount. Specifically, some of the foods allowed are;

➤ **Vegetables:**

Nothing is better than a meal prepared with fresh vegetables. Vegetables are the key to a healthy life in a vegetarian lifestyle because, they are a great source of fiber, iron, sodium, potassium, minerals, and vitamins that greatly help in controlling body weight and lowering risks of cardiac diseases.
Portion: Have 4 servings of vegetables per day, about 1 cup of raw veggies or 1/2 cup cooked. Ensure to have one calcium-rich green vegetable on your plate like spinach or kale.

➤ **Fruits:**

The main focus of a vegetarian meal is in the vegetables and fruits because, fruits are ample in antioxidant that helps in strengthening the immune system of the body that also provides vitamins, minerals and other essential nutrients to the body.
Portion: Have 3 servings of fruits per day, about 1/2 cup of chopped fruit. Ensure the fruit is low in calories like berries, mangoes, oranges, grapefruits and kiwis.

➤ **Whole grains:**

Increase the portion of iron, fiber, and antioxidant in your meal by adding grains to your plate. Ensure that you take in vegetarian foods containing quinoa, oats, barley and even popcorn.
Portion: Have 8 serving per day, about 1 cup of uncooked or 1/2 cup of cooked grains, or a slice of whole-grain bread.

- **Legumes and lentils:**

  Legumes and lentils are an excellent source of protein and fiber. They also contain a good amount of vitamin, zinc, and iron. The best thing about legumes and lentils is that, they increase in volume during cooking, therefore you can have them as much as you desire without counting the amount of calories taken in.
  Portion: Have 3 servings per day, about 1 cup of uncooked or 1/2 cup of cooked beans or lentils.

- **Eggs and dairy products:**

  Lacto vegetarian and ovo-lacto vegetarians can use eggs and dairy products. They are packed with vitamin B, calcium and protein that are essential for strengthening the teeth and bones respectively. Also, they are a great replacement for legumes and lentils
  Portions: Have 1 cup of milk or 1-ounce of meat substitute daily.

- **Soy foods:**

  Not only vegans, other kinds of vegetarians can also use this amazing meat substitute called the soy foods. Soy foods are rich in amino acids, protein, omega3 fatty acids, zinc, and iron. Example of soy foods are the tofu, seitan, tempeh and the soybeans. The best thing about them is that they can pair up with any ingredient.
  Portion: Have 3 servings per day, about 1 cup.

- **Nuts and seeds:**

  Complete your meal with walnuts, peanuts, almonds and cashews. These nuts and seeds like the chia seeds and flax seeds are high in good saturated fats and calories. Instead of increasing weights, nuts and seeds help in reducing weight and controlling the cholesterol levels. Also endeavor to use seeds and nuts in your breakfast, soups and bread.
  Portion: Have 2 servings per day, about 1/4 cup.

Foods to Avoid

Here are some foods that should be either used moderately in the vegetarian or shouldn't be used at all.

Sugar:

Sugar is a big "no" in a vegetarian diet because, it doesn't have any nutrients, therefore making its calories harmful to the body. Furthermore, sugar increases the risk of dental problems, diabetes and high cholesterol level which contributes to the weakening of one's metabolism. Substituting sugar with fruits or vegetarian alternatives like almond sugar, coconut sugar, maple syrup, honey or applesauce would be much better.

> **Gelatin based foods:**

Gelatin is a thickening agent which is an animal by-product. Since it is an animal based food, gelatin should be avoided in the vegetarian diet, meaning, one should always try to avoid the use of sour cream, cottage cheese and margarine when carrying out a vegetarian diet.

> **Egg and dairy products:**

Even though eggs and dairy-products are allowed to be use in some kinds of vegetarian diets, nevertheless, always ensure that they are used moderately. Eggs, milk and products made from these foods are high in saturated fats and cholesterol which is often harmful to one's health. These foods increase the risk of cardiac diseases, therefore it is advisable for one to use them in little proportions and when necessary.

It is also advisable to make gradual changes in becoming a vegetarian. Though one can switch to a vegetarian lifestyle in a jiffy, there are some loopholes like digestion problems, bloating, fatigue and feelings of low energy that may await you. Therefore, taking a gradual and meticulous transition towards becoming a vegetarian will certainly reduce the presence of these impacts. Start the transition with a no-meat recipe, replace the meat recipes with meat substitutes and then continue to make changes with the ingredient until it transforms into a vegetarian diet. Certainly, any meal can be transformed in a vegetarian diet using meat substitutes or meat and dairy products in moderation, along with fresh vegetables, fruits, millets, legumes, beans and grains.

On following this, you will learn some skills in cooking a vegetarian meal, as the recipes are divided into 10 collections: breakfast, lunch, dinner, side dishes, bread, soups, stews, sauces, chilies, desserts and drinks.

You will also find a flavorful, appealing variety of the vegetarian dishes that will help you get started and also maintain your vegetarian lifestyle. The major cooking utensil used in the preparation of these dishes is the slow cooker because, it makes cooking smart in what should be a tedious lifestyle.

Read on to learn more about the slow cooker.

Chapter 2: Why Use the Slow Cooker?

The slow cooker is a cheap and smart countertop cooker that promotes remote form of cooking. It is a perfect kitchen appliance for healthy and low-fat meals like vegetarian meals. Also, it is a blessing and a life saver for cooks who are extremely occupied and busy to cook large hearty meals with minimal efforts. This cooker can be adjusted to cook before leaving for work without losing its quality of taste and sumptuousness at the end of the day. Furthermore, using a single pot to prepare foods reduces water usage in cleaning, and this is where the slow cooker crock is much better. Another advantage of the slow cooker is that it brings out the flavors in foods, I mean any food. Yes, any food recipe can be modified to prepare it in the slow cooker therefore; slow cookers offers a wide food variety of food like soups, stews, sauces, beverages, desserts and even bread. I mean, what's not there to love about a slow cooker?

Basic Knowledge about the Slow Cooker

During the 1970s when women started working, the use of slow cookers started gaining popularity in America. It helped working women in such a way that, they could just place the ingredients for their dinner in the slow cooker before leaving to their various work places, and then adjust the time for everything to be processed, so that they will get home to see their already prepared dinner. Also it is important to note that with slow cooking at a low temperature, it is impossible for foods to burn or neither is there a need for a constant monitoring of the heating levels and stirring contents. All that is required of you, is just to throw in all the ingredients in the slow cooker, adjust the heat setting, cooking time and leave the rest to the slow cooker. That notwithstanding, discoveries have made it clear that although the appliance can work remotely, cooks often do hesitate to leave the slow cooker on cooking while away from their home. For this, it is recommended to cook your food when you are at home or while you are sleeping.

Benefits of the Slow Cooker

1. Time-saving:

The slow cooker is best for cooks who run a short time routine like in the morning. In this respect, all one has to do is to, prepare the ingredients ahead and store it in the refrigerator for the night. Then in the next morning, let the content rest on the counter top at a room temperature for 20 minutes and then add it to the slow cooker. The same goes for preparing breakfast. Prepare the contents, add it to the slow cooker at night, set it to cook throughout the night and have a warm healthy breakfast in the morning. Cook foods in the slow cooker that needs less pre-preparation or uses raw ingredients.

2. Low in fat and flavorful food

Slow cooker gives healthier and tasty result to meals because; the ingredients placed into it are often fresh. Also the slow cookers don't need oil to prevent the catching of food as this is automatically prevented by the cooking liquid. Light greasing with a non-stick cooking spray can work if it is necessary to use oil for the preparation of the food. Furthermore, the long cooking time allows the vegetables and other contents to attain fuller flavors.

3. All season appliance

The slow cooker is suitable for cooking at any time of the year. Serve warming soups and stew on a cold day or use it in the summer time to remove the discomfort of the stove or oven heat in the kitchen.

4. Energy efficient

This electronic appliance is very economical and uses less energy compared to an electric oven.

5. Easy to transport

The slow cooker is very convenient to carry because; you can take warming food to eat elsewhere without reheating.

How the Slow Cooker Works

The cooking principle of the slow cooker is gentle simmering or boiling of food at a low temperature. Thus, the design of the slow cooker contains three parts: a removable crock made up of ceramic, heat housing with controls and a lid.

1- **Ceramic crock:** A glazed pot or crock of the slow cooker has a ceramic ingredient, as it is spherical in shape. The capacity of the slow cooker depends on the size and space of the crock, if small, medium or large slow-cooker.
2- **Heat housing:** A metal heating pot that houses the crock and contains an electric heating element in the bottom. The manual or programed controller in the slow cooker allows the users to cook conveniently at any of the two heat settings which are the low heat setting or high heat setting. Exclusively, some slow cookers also come with the option of an average and keep warm setting.

3- **Lid**: The lid being made of glass, prevents spillage of contents in the crock during cooking, collects condensed vapors, prevents warmth from escaping the top and maintains a low-pressure for sealing. It is positioned on the edge of the pot in such a way that it poses no form of danger, in case of a sudden pressure release like in the pressure cooker.

Cooking in the slow cooker involves one-step preparation and this involves assembling the raw or precooked ingredients all at once into the crock and then submerging them into the cooking liquid like water or stock. Close the cooker with its lid, plug in to turn on and select the heat setting from the controls. When that is done, the heating element will start heating and warming the cooking liquid that will ultimately warm the food in the crock. At a high heat setting, the temperature of the food will rise until it reaches the boiling point and then at this point, the gentle boiling of the food will begin, while at a low heat setting, the food gently simmers below the boiling point temperature. During the cooking processes in the crockpot, the condensation collected on the bottom of the lid returns back to the food. Now the question arises, how long should the food be cooked in the slow cooker?

➢ For meals taking 15 to 30 minutes time to cook on a stove top, cook it in the slow cooker for 1 to 2 hours on a high heat setting or 4 to 6 hours on a low heat setting.
➢ For meals taking 30 to 60 minutes time to cook on stove top, cook it in the slow cooker for 2 to 3 hours on a high heat setting or 5 to 7 hours on a low heat setting.
➢ For meals taking 1 to 2 hours' time to cook on stove top, cook it in the slow cooker for 3 to 4 hours on a high heat setting or 6 to 8 hours on a low heat setting.
➢ For meal taking 2 to 4 hours' time to cook on stove top, cook it in the slow cooker for 4 to 6 hours on a high heat setting or 8 to 12 hours on a low heat setting.

In general, adjust the heat setting for the time you want the food to cook, but always remember that slow cooking for two hours at a low heat setting is equal to slow cooking for 1 hour at high cooking setting.

The 8 Dos When Using Your Slow Cooker

1- Use the right size of slow cooker. The size available for the slow cooker is from 1 to 8 quarts. Use 4 quarts slow cooker for cooking food for 4 people or preparing sauces and then a size of 6 to 8 quarts slow cooker when preparing a meal for more than five people or when you want leftovers.

2- When converting a regular recipe to the slow cooker recipe, reduce the cooking liquid like water, milk, broth or sauces by one-half to one-third as the liquid in the slow cooking doesn't boil.

3- In the vegetarian recipes, place the vegetables at the bottom of the cooker as they often take longer cooking time to turn soft.

4- Fill the cooker with no more than two-thirds of the contents and the cooking liquid. Also the volume of the food affects the cooking time, taste and quality.

5- To make sure that the contents in the cooker are cooked thoroughly, for the first hour set the heat setting to high and cook the remaining hours on a low heat setting.

6- Add the grains like rice or pasta at the end of a cooking time, like during the last 60 to 30 minutes, or just add them separately.

7- Pour in milk or dairy products like cream or cheese when the last hour of cooking starts, to prevent curdling of these food items.

8- You may also add soft vegetables like zucchini and tomatoes like during the last 30 to 45 minutes.

The 4 Don'ts When Using Your Slow Cooker

1- Don't add frozen foods directly into the slow cooker. The frozen food needs more cooking time and increases the risk of food disorderliness in the meal. Let frozen food item dissolve at a room temperature before adding to the slow cooker.

2- Don't stir frequently and open the top because, every time the top is removed, some of the heat escapes from the cooker, resulting in it taking more time, approximately 30 minutes to attain the set cooking temperature. If necessary, stir halfway through the cooking time.

3- Don't fill the slow cooker with the cooking liquid because, vegetables and fruits will release their own liquid during the cooking process. Furthermore, adding too much liquid will take more cooking time for its boiling and will prevent its evaporation. If there is too much liquid in the slow cooker, continue cooking for 2 hours or until the liquid reduces to the desired level,before you can uncover the cover.

4- Don't cool off the hot food in the crock of the slow cooker because, the crockpot is meant to retain the warmth of the food. In order to cool the food, transfer it to another bowl.

Foods Compatible with the Slower Cooker

The slow cooker is known for enhancing the flavors of foods, especially for the meat and vegetables. This is due to the long cooking time that allows contents to absorb the spices and nutrients in the broth and sauce. A variety of food can be prepared using the slow cooker.

1- Soups, chili, and stews:

One of the best slow cooker meals are soups, chili and stews. Soups and stews need long simmering time on a low heat and this is one of the prominent features of the slow cooker. Place ingredients in the slow cooker, preferably raw and then cover it with cooking liquid like water or broth, preferably boiled and let it cook.

2- Whole-grain meals:

Have a warming and nutritious breakfast without much effort in the morning by cooking grains like oats or rice porridge in the slow cooker overnight.

3- Sauces:

You can prepare mouthwatering sauces in the slow cooker, as the low heat brings out the flavor and texture in the sauce without any form of burning.

4- Bread and Pizzas:

Slow cooker surprisingly works properly in baking bread and pizzas as well, as the low heat helps the dough of bread and pizza to rise.

5- Desserts:

Slow cooking also functions properly in the preparation of desserts. Use the slow cooker to prepare heavenly fruit desserts and even delicious cakes.

6- Drinks:

Nourish your body with tempting and soothing drinks by preparing them in the slow cooker. Slow cook drinks and have it anytime of the day.

Maintenance of the Slow Cooker

Slow cooker needs little maintenance compared to other electrical kitchen appliances. All you just have to do is to;
- ➢ Avoid placing its hot top into wet, cold surfaces or water.
- ➢ Avoid hitting the crock or lid against hard surfaces.
- ➢ Avoid using the crock of the slow cooker for refrigerating or storing purposes, as it may damage the crock.
- ➢ Avoid using damaged lid or crock for cooking.
- ➢ Always contact the service provider for any other service.
- ➢ Clean the slow cooker regularly.

The slow cooker is a blessing for those who have no time to cook a healthy food, as it is very easy to clean as well. Don't worry about cleaning the slow cooker because, you don't have to be on duty for that, doing an all-night scrubbing. Moreover, make sure to grease the crock of the slow cooker with a non-stick cooking spray before cooking. For cleaning a slow cooker, you will need a;
- ➢ Baking soda
- ➢ Apple cider vinegar
- ➢ Cotton cloth
- ➢ Dish soup

Instructions:

1- Prepare a mixture of the baking soda and vinegar.
2- Unplug the slow cooker, then soak the cotton cloth in the warm water and wipe the exterior body parts.
3- Using a screw driver, remove the handles, knobs, the top and then clean them individually with the warm soapy water.
4- For removing stains on the exterior body, top, handles, knobs, apply the baking soda mixture to it.
5- Remove the crock from the slow cooker and wash it in the dish washer.
6- If dish washing the crock isn't removing the tough stains, fill the crock with water, pour and stir in 2 tablespoons of the baking soda and 1 tablespoons of dish soap. Then let it cook on the low heating setting for several hours until the stains come off. Thereafter clean the crock in the dish washer.
7- Clean the area of the heating element with a damp cloth only, but don't submerge it with water and let it cool off completely before cleaning.

Chapter 3: 101 Vegetarian Slow Cooker Recipes

GREAT BREAKFAST

1. Ultra Decadent Breakfast Potatoes

Yield: 6 (about 10 cups)
Total time: 3 hours and 15 minutes
Ingredients:

- 2 tablespoons of unsalted butter, grated
- 2 tablespoons of olive oil
- 3 pounds of red baby potatoes
- 1 medium-sized green bell pepper, cored
- 1 medium-sized red bell pepper, cored
- 1/2 cup of diced white onion
- 1 1/2 teaspoon of minced garlic
- 2 1/2 teaspoons of salt
- 3/4 teaspoon of ground black pepper
- 2 teaspoons of smoked paprika

Directions:

1. Take a 6-quart slow cooker and grease the bottom with a non-stick cooking spray.
2. Rinse the potatoes, dice it into 1 1/2 inch pieces and add it to the slow cooker.
3. Cut the bell peppers into 1 1/2 inch pieces and add it to the slow cooker along with the remaining ingredients.
4. Stir it until it is properly combined and cover the top.
5. Plug in the slow cooker, adjust the cooking time to 3 hours and let it cook at a high heat setting or until the potatoes are soft to be picked by a fork.
6. When the potatoes are done, add the seasoning and serve.

Nutrition Value:
Calories:192 Cal, Carbohydrates:32g, Protein:4g, Fats:6g, Fiber:3g.

2. Cozy Oatmeal with Cinnamon & Apple

Yield: 10
Total time: 5 hours and 15 minutes
Ingredients:

- 1 tablespoon of melted coconut oil
- 1 cup of steel cut oats
- 2 medium-sized apples, peeled, cored and diced
- 1/2 teaspoon of salt
- 1 teaspoon of cinnamon
- 2 tablespoons of brown sugar
- ¼ cup of chopped walnuts
- 12 fluid ounce of coconut milk, unsweetened
- 12 fluid ounce of water

Directions:

1. Take a 6-quart slow cooker and grease the bottom with a non-stick cooking spray.
2. Add all the ingredients except for the almonds into the slow cooker and stir until it is properly mixed.
3. Cover the top, plug in the slow cooker, adjust the cooking time to 5 hours and let it cook on alow heat setting or until it cooks thoroughly.
4. Garnish it with the almonds and serve.

Nutrition Value:
Calories:192 Cal, Carbohydrates:32g, Protein:4g, Fats:6g, Fiber:3g.

3. Mouthwatering Breakfast Quinoa

Yield: 8
Total time: 3 hours and 5 minutes
Ingredients:

- 1 cup of quinoa
- 1 medium-sized apple, peeled and diced
- 4 dates, chopped
- 1/4 cup of pumpkin seeds, shelled
- 3 cups of almond milk, unsweetened
- 1/4 teaspoon of salt
- 2 teaspoons of ground cinnamon
- 1/4 teaspoon of ground nutmeg
- 1 teaspoon of vanilla extract, unsweetened

Directions:

1. Take a 6-quart slow cooker and grease the bottom with a non-stick cooking spray.
2. Add all the ingredients into the slow cooker and stir until it mixes properly.
3. Cover the top, plug in the slow cooker, adjust the cooking time to 2 hours and let cook on a high heat setting or until the quinoa absorbs all the cooking liquid.
4. Serve right away.

Nutrition Value:
Calories:335 Cal, Carbohydrates:59g, Protein:10g, Fats:7.3g, Fiber:6g.

4. Heavenly Chocolate Oatmeal

Yield: 8
Total time: 6 hours and 5 minutes
Ingredients:

- 16-ounce of steel cut oats
- 1/4 cup of cocoa powder, unsweetened
- 4 tablespoons of brown sugar
- 2 tablespoons of chopped pecans
- 1 tablespoon of shredded coconut
- 14 fluid ounce of coconut milk, unsweetened
- 7 cups of water

Directions:

1. Take a 6-quart slow cooker and grease the bottom with a non-stick cooking spray.
2. Add the oats cocoa powder, milk, water into the slow cooker and stir until it mixes properly.
3. Cover the top, plug in the slow cooker, adjust the cooking time to 6 hours and let it cook on a low heat setting or until it cooks thoroughly.
4. Sprinkle it with sugar, top it with the pecans, coconut and serve right away.

Nutrition Value:

Calories:370 Cal, Carbohydrates:70g, Protein:8.4g, Fats:4.5g, Fiber:8.8g.

5. *Scrumptious Spinach and Mushrooms Quiche*

Yield: 6
Total time: 4 hours and 15 minutes
Ingredients:

- 14-ounce of firm tofu, pressed and drained
- 10-ounce of frozen spinach, thawed and drained
- 8-ounce of sliced mushrooms
- 1/2 cup of diced white onion
- 1 teaspoon of minced garlic
- 2 tablespoons of nutritional yeast
- 1/4 teaspoon of dried basil
- 1/4 teaspoon of dried thyme
- 1 teaspoon of salt
- 1/4 teaspoon of red pepper flakes
- 1/2 teaspoon of ground black pepper
- 1 teaspoon of lemon zest
- 1 tablespoon of olive oil
- 1 tablespoon of lemon juice
- 1 tablespoon of apple cider vinegar

Directions:

1. Take a 6-quart slow cooker; grease the bottom with a non-stick cooking spray and set it aside until when it is needed.
2. Place a medium-sized skillet pan over an average temperature of heat, add the oil and let it heat until it gets hot.
3. Add the onion, garlic, spinach, mushrooms and cook for 5 to 8 minutes or until it gets softened.
4. Drain the moisture and stir in the salt, black pepper, red pepper flakes, basil and thyme.
5. Scoop this mixture into the slow cooker.
6. Using a food processor, place the tofu, lemon zest, lemon juice, vinegar and pulse until it gets smooth.
7. Turn this mixture into the slow cooker, add the nutritional yeast and stir until it combines properly.
8. Cover the top, plug in the slow cooker; adjust the cooking time to 4 hours and let it steam on a low heat setting or until it is set.
9. Serve right away.

Nutrition Value:
Calories: 440 Cal, Carbohydrates:39g, Protein:14g, Fats:20g, Fiber:4g.

6. Nutritious Chocolate & Cherry Oatmeal

Yield: 5
Total time: 8 hours and 10 minutes
Ingredients:

- 1 cup of steel cut oats
- 1/3 cup of dried tart cherries
- 1 1/2 cups of frozen tart cherries
- 2 tablespoons of cocoa powder, unsweetened
- 1 ounce of chopped chocolate, unsweetened
- 1/8 teaspoon of salt
- 1/4 cup of maple syrup
- 3/4 teaspoon of almond extract, divided
- 16 fluid ounce of almond milk, unsweetened
- 2 cups and 2 tablespoons of water, divided

Directions:

1. Take a 6-quart slow cooker; grease the bottom with a non-stick cooking spray and set it aside until it is called for.
2. Add the oats, dried cherries, cocoa powder, chocolate, salt, maple syrup, 1/2 teaspoon of almond extract, milk and 2 cups of water.
3. Stir it until it mixes properly and cover the top.
4. Plug in the slow cooker; adjust the cooking time to 4 hours and let it cook on a low heat setting or until it is done.
5. In the meantime, place a small saucepan over an average heat and add the remaining ingredients.
6. Stir until it mixes properly and let it cook for 7 to 10 minutes or until the sauce is thickened slightly.
7. When the oats are done, stir and if the mixture is thick pour in 2 to 3 tablespoons of milk.
8. Divide the oats evenly into serving bowls, top it with the prepared sauce and serve.

Nutrition Value:
Calories: 103 Cal, Carbohydrates:3.6g, Protein:2g, Fats:4g, Fiber:1g.

7. Convenient Scrambled Tofu Burritos

Yield: 4
Total time: 4 to 8 hours
Ingredients:

- 8 ounces of tofu, crumbled
- 15 ounces of cooked black beans
- 1 small white onion, peeled and chopped
- 2 tablespoons of green pepper, minced
- 1 cup of shredded lettuce
- 1 medium-sized avocado, cored and sliced
- 1/2 teaspoon of salt
- 1/2 teaspoon of ground black pepper
- 1/4 teaspoon of red chili powder
- 1/2 teaspoon of ground turmeric
- 1/4 teaspoon of ground cumin
- 1/4 teaspoon of smoked paprika
- 1/2 cup of tomato salsa
- 3/4 cup of water
- 1/2 cup of shredded vegan Parmesan cheese
- 4 whole-wheat tortillas, warmed

Directions:

1. Using an 8 quarts slow cooker, place the tofu, beans, onion, green pepper, salt, black pepper, red chili powder, turmeric, cumin, paprika and water.
2. Stir until it mixes properly and cover the top.
3. Plug in slow cooker; adjust the cooking time to 8 hours and let it steam on a low heat setting or until it is cooked thoroughly.
4. When the beans are cooked thoroughly, pour in the salt, black pepper and mix properly.
5. Working on one tortilla at a time, scoop 1/4 portion of the beans mixture, top it with 2 tablespoons of each salsa, cheese, lettuce and avocado slices.
6. Roll up and serve.

Nutrition Value:
Calories:118 Cal, Carbohydrates:20g, Protein:6g, Fats:2g, Fiber:3g.

8. Crunchy Apple Granola Crumble

Yield: 6
Total time: 4 hours and 15 minutes
Ingredients:

- 1/2 cup of granola
- 1/2 cup of bran flakes
- 2 medium-sized apples, peeled, cored and diced
- 1/2 teaspoon of ground nutmeg
- 1 teaspoon of ground cinnamon
- 2 tablespoon of peanut butter
- 2 tablespoons of maple syrup
- 1/4 cup of apple juice

Directions:

1. Take a 6-quart slow cooker and grease the bottom with a non-stick cooking spray.
2. Add all the ingredients into the slow cooker and stir until it is properly combined.
3. Cover the top, plug in the slow cooker, adjust the cooking time to 4 hours and let it steam on a high heat setting or until it is done.
4. Serve right away.

Nutrition Value:
Calories: 369 Cal, Carbohydrates: 56g, Protein: 5g, Fats: 15g, Fiber: 5g.

9. Satisfying Wild Rice Breakfast Porridge

Yield: 8
Total time: 3 hours and 5 minutes
Ingredients:

- 1 1/2 cups of wild rice
- 1/2 cup of chopped walnuts
- 2/3 cup of dried cranberries
- 1/2 cup of pecans, toasted and roughly chopped
- 1 teaspoon of salt
- 1 teaspoon of ground cinnamon
- 3 cups of water
- 8 fluid ounce of milk and more for serving

Directions:

1. Using a 6-quarts slow cooker, place the rice, cranberries, salt and milk.
2. Stir until it is combined properly and cover the top.
3. Plug in the slow cooker, adjust the cooking time to 4 hours and let it cook on low heat setting or until the rice absorbs all the cooking liquid.
4. When the porridge is done, pour in the nuts, cinnamon, maple syrup and serve it with more milk.

Nutrition Value:
Calories:553 Cal, Carbohydrates:59g, Protein:10g, Fats:33g, Fiber:5g.

10. Spectacular Pumpkin Butter

Yield: 16
Total time: 5 hours and 5 minutes
Ingredients:

- 30-ounce of pumpkin purée
- 1 teaspoon of ground ginger
- 2 teaspoon of ground cinnamon
- 1/2 teaspoon of ground nutmeg
- 1 1/4 cup of maple syrup
- 1 teaspoon of vanilla extract, unsweetened

Directions:

1. Using a bowl whisk together the pumpkin puree, maple syrup and vanilla until it is properly combined.
2. Add this mixture into a 6 quarts slow cooker and cover the top.
3. Plug in the slow cooker; adjust the cooking time to 4 hours and let it steam on a high heat setting.
4. When the last hour of cooking draws near, pour in the remaining ingredients until it mixes properly.
5. When butter is ready, let it cool off completely, store it in sterilized jars or serve right away.

Nutrition Value:
Calories:40 Cal, Carbohydrates:0g, Protein:0g, Fats:0g, Fiber:0g.

DELICIOUS LUNCH

1. Hearty Black Lentil Curry

Yield: 4
Total time: 6 hours and 35 minutes
Ingredients:

- 1 cup of black lentils, rinsed and soaked overnight
- 14 ounce of chopped tomatoes
- 2 large white onions, peeled and sliced
- 1 1/2 teaspoon of minced garlic
- 1 teaspoon of grated ginger
- 1 red chili
- 1 teaspoon of salt
- 1/4 teaspoon of red chili powder
- 1 teaspoon of paprika
- 1 teaspoon of ground turmeric
- 2 teaspoons of ground cumin
- 2 teaspoons of ground coriander
- 1/2 cup of chopped coriander
- 4-ounce of vegetarian butter
- 4 fluid of ounce water
- 2 fluid of ounce vegetarian double cream

Directions:

1. Place a large pan over an average heat, add butter and let heat until melt.
2. Add the onion along with garlic and ginger and let cook for 10 to 15 minutes or until onions are caramelized.
3. Then stir in salt, red chili powder, paprika, turmeric, cumin, ground coriander, and water.
4. Transfer this mixture to a 6-quarts slow cooker and add tomatoes and red chili.
5. Drain lentils, add to slow cooker and stir until just mix.
6. Plug in slow cooker; adjust cooking time to 6 hours and let cook on low heat setting.
7. When the lentils are done, stir in cream and adjust the seasoning.
8. Serve with boiled rice or whole wheat bread.

Nutrition Value:
Calories:527 Cal, Carbohydrates:35g, Protein:19g, Fats:34g, Fiber:6g.

2. *Flavorful Refried Beans*

Yield: 8
Total time: 8 hours and 15 minutes
Ingredients:

- 3 cups of pinto beans, rinsed
- 1 small jalapeno pepper, seeded and chopped
- 1 medium-sized white onion, peeled and sliced
- 2 tablespoons of minced garlic
- 5 teaspoons of salt
- 2 teaspoons of ground black pepper
- 1/4 teaspoon of ground cumin
- 9 cups of water

Directions:

1. Using a 6-quarts slow cooker, place all the ingredients and stir until it mixes properly.
2. Cover the top, plug in the slow cooker; adjust the cooking time to 6 hours, let it cook on high heat setting and add more water if the beans get too dry.
3. When the beans are done, drain them and reserve the liquid.
4. Mash the beans using a potato masher and pour in the reserved cooking liquid until it reaches your desired mixture.
5. Serve immediately.

Nutrition Value:
Calories: 105 Cal, Carbohydrates: 36g, Protein:13g, Fats:1g, Fiber:13g.

3. Smoky Red Beans and Rice

Yield: 6
Total time: 5 hours and 10 minutes
Ingredients:

- 30 ounce of cooked red beans
- 1 cup of brown rice, uncooked
- 1 cup of chopped green pepper
- 1 cup of chopped celery
- 1 cup of chopped white onion
- 1 1/2 teaspoon of minced garlic
- 1/2 teaspoon of salt
- 1/4 teaspoon of cayenne pepper
- 1 teaspoon of smoked paprika
- 2 teaspoons of dried thyme
- 1 bay leaf
- 2 1/3 cups of vegetable broth

Directions:

1. Using a 6-quarts slow cooker place all the ingredients except for the rice, salt and cayenne pepper.
2. Stir until it mixes properly and then cover the top.
3. Plug in the slow cooker; adjust the cooking time to 4 hours and let it steam on a low heat setting.
4. Then pour in and stir the rice, salt, cayenne pepper and continue cooking for an additional 2 hours at a high heat setting.
5. Serve straight away.

Nutrition Value:
Calories:425 Cal, Carbohydrates:62g, Protein:27g, Fats:22g, Fiber:15g.

4. Spicy Black-Eyed Peas

Yield: 8
Total time: 8 hours and 20 minutes
Ingredients:

- 32-ounce black-eyed peas, uncooked
- 1 cup of chopped orange bell pepper
- 1 cup of chopped celery
- 8-ounce of chipotle peppers, chopped
- 1 cup of chopped carrot
- 1 cup of chopped white onion
- 1 teaspoon of minced garlic
- 3/4 teaspoon of salt
- 1/2 teaspoon of ground black pepper
- 2 teaspoons of liquid smoke flavoring
- 2 teaspoons of ground cumin
- 1 tablespoon of adobo sauce
- 2 tablespoons of olive oil
- 1 tablespoon of apple cider vinegar
- 4 cups of vegetable broth

Directions:

1. Place a medium-sized non-stick skillet pan over an average temperature of heat; add the bell peppers, carrot, onion, garlic, oil and vinegar.
2. Stir until it mixes properly and let it cook for 5 to 8 minutes or until it gets translucent.
3. Transfer this mixture to a 6-quarts slow cooker and add the peas, chipotle pepper, adobo sauce and the vegetable broth.
4. Stir until mixes properly and cover the top.
5. Plug in the slow cooker; adjust the cooking time to 8 hours and let it cook on the low heat setting or until peas are soft.
6. Serve right away.

Nutrition Value:
Calories:165 Cal, Carbohydrates:23g, Protein:6.7g, Fats:2.5g, Fiber:3.7g.

5. Chunky Black Lentil Veggie Soup

Yield: 8
Total time: 4 hours and 35 minutes
Ingredients:

- 1 1/2 cups of black lentils, uncooked
- 2 small turnips, peeled and diced
- 10 medium-sized carrots, peeled and diced
- 1 medium-sized green bell pepper, cored and diced
- 3 cups of diced tomatoes
- 1 medium-sized white onion, peeled and diced
- 2 tablespoons of minced ginger
- 1 teaspoon of minced garlic
- 1 teaspoon of salt
- 1/2 teaspoon of ground coriander
- 1/2 teaspoon of ground cumin
- 3 tablespoons of unsalted butter
- 32 fluid ounce of vegetable broth
- 32 fluid ounce of water

Directions:

1. Using a medium-sized microwave, cover the bowl, place the lentils and pour in the water.
2. Microwave lentils for 10 minutes or until softened, stirring after 5 minutes.
3. Drain lentils and add to a 6-quarts slow cooker along with remaining ingredients and stir until just mix.
4. Cover with top, plug in slow cooker; adjust cooking time to 6 hours and let cook on low heat setting or until carrots are tender.
5. Serve straight away.

Nutrition Value:

Calories:90 Cal, Carbohydrates:15g, Protein:3g, Fats:2g, Fiber:3g.

6. Exotic Butternut Squash and Chickpea Curry

Yield: 8
Total time: 6 hours and 15 minutes
Ingredients:

- 1 1/2 cups of shelled peas
- 1 1/2 cups of chick peas, uncooked and rinsed
- 2 1/2 cups of diced butternut squash
- 12 ounce of chopped spinach
- 2 large tomatoes, diced
- 1 small white onion, peeled and chopped
- 1 teaspoon of minced garlic
- 1 teaspoon of salt
- 3 tablespoons of curry powder
- 14-ounce of coconut milk
- 3 cups of vegetable broth
- 1/4 cup of chopped cilantro

Directions:

1. Using a 6-quarts slow cooker, place all the ingredients into it except for the spinach and peas.
2. Cover the top, plug in the slow cooker; adjust the cooking time to 6 hours and let it cook on the high heat setting or until the chickpeas get tender.
3. 30 minutes to ending your cooking, add the peas and spinach to the slow cooker and let it cook for the remaining 30 minutes.
4. Stir to check the sauce, if the sauce is runny, stir in a mixture of a tablespoon of cornstarch mixed with 2 tablespoons of water.
5. Serve with boiled rice.

Nutrition Value:
Calories:243 Cal, Carbohydrates:46g, Protein:8g, Fats:5.5g, Fiber:11.6g.

7. Sizzling Vegetarian Fajitas

Yield: 8
Total time:
Ingredients:

- 4 ounce of diced green chilies
- 3 medium-sized tomatoes, diced
- 1 large green bell pepper, cored and sliced
- 1 large red bell pepper, cored and sliced
- 1 medium-sized white onion, peeled and sliced
- 1/2 teaspoon of garlic powder
- 1/4 teaspoon of salt
- 2 teaspoons of red chili powder
- 2 teaspoons of ground cumin
- 1/2 teaspoon of dried oregano
- 1 1/2 tablespoon of olive oil

Directions:

1. Take a 6-quarts slow cooker, grease it with a non-stick cooking spray and add all the ingredients.
2. Stir until it mixes properly and cover the top.
3. Plug in the slow cooker; adjust the cooking time to 2 hours and let it cook on the high heat setting or until cooks thoroughly.
4. Serve with tortillas.

Nutrition Value:
Calories:220 Cal, Carbohydrates:73g, Protein:12g, Fats:8g, Fiber:4g.

8. Rich Red Lentil Curry

Yield: 16
Total time: 8 hours and 10 minutes
Ingredients:

- 4 cups of brown lentils, uncooked and rinsed
- 2 medium-sized white onions, peeled and diced
- 2 teaspoons of minced garlic
- 1 tablespoon of minced ginger
- 1 teaspoon of salt
- 1/4 teaspoon of cayenne pepper
- 5 tablespoons of red curry paste
- 2 teaspoon of brown sugar
- 1 1/2 teaspoon of ground turmeric
- 1 tablespoon of garam masala
- 60-ounce of tomato puree
- 7 cups of water
- 1/2 cup of coconut milk
- 1/4 cup of chopped cilantro

Directions:

1. Using a 6-quarts slow cooker, place all the ingredients except for the coconut milk and cilantro.
2. Stir until it mixes properly and cover the top.
3. Plug in the slow cooker; adjust the cooking time to 5 hours and let it cook on the high heat setting or until the lentils are soft.
4. Check the curry during cooking and add more water if needed.
5. When the curry is cooked, stir in the milk, then garnish it with the cilantro and serve right away.

Nutrition Value:
Calories:192 Cal, Carbohydrates:33g, Protein:12g, Fats:3g, Fiber:11g.

9. Lovely Parsnip & Split Pea Soup

Yield: 8
Total time: 5 hours and 10 minutes
Ingredients:

- 1 tablespoon of olive oil
- 2 large parsnips, peeled and chopped
- 2 large carrots, peeled and chopped
- 1 medium-sized white onion, peeled and diced
- 1 1/2 teaspoon of minced garlic
- 2 1/4 cups of dried green split peas, rinsed
- 1 teaspoon of salt
- 1/2 teaspoon of ground black pepper
- 1 teaspoon of dried thyme
- 2 bay leaves
- 6 cups of vegetable broth
- 1 teaspoon of liquid smoke

Directions:

1. Place a medium-sized non-stick skillet pan over an average pressure of heat, add the oil and let it heat.
2. Add the parsnip, carrot, onion, garlic and let it cook for 5 minutes or until it is heated.
3. Transfer this mixture into a 6-quarts slow cooker and add the remaining ingredients.
4. Stir until mixes properly and cover the top.
5. Plug in the slow cooker; adjust the cooking time to 5 hours and let it cook on the high heat setting or until the peas and vegetables get soft.
6. When done, remove the bay leaf from the soup and blend it with a submersion blender or until the soup reaches your desired state.
7. Add the seasoning and serve.

Nutrition Value:
Calories:199 Cal, Carbohydrates:21g, Protein:18g, Fats:5g, Fiber:8g.

10. Incredible Tomato Basil Soup

Yield: 6
Total time: 6 hours and 10 minutes
Ingredients:

- 1 cup of chopped celery
- 1 cup of chopped carrots
- 74 ounce of whole tomatoes, canned
- 2 cups of chopped white onion
- 2 teaspoons of minced garlic
- 1 tablespoon of salt
- 1/2 teaspoon of ground white pepper
- 1/4 cup of basil leaves and more for garnishing
- 1 bay leaf
- 32 fluid ounce of vegetable broth
- 1/2 cup of grated Parmesan cheese

Directions:

1. Using an 8 quarts or larger slow cooker, place all the ingredients.
2. Stir until it mixes properly and cover the top.
3. Plug in the slow cooker; adjust the cooking time to 5 hours and let it cook on the high heat setting or until the vegetables are tender.
4. Blend the soup with a submersion blender or until soup reaches your desired state.
5. Garnish it with the cheese, basil leaves and serve.

Nutrition Value:
Calories:210 Cal, Carbohydrates:11g, Protein:12g, Fats:10g, Fiber:3g.

FLAVORED DINNER

1. Savory Spanish Rice

Yield: 10
Total time: 3 hours and 10 minutes
Ingredients:

- 1 cup of long grain rice, uncooked
- 1/2 cup of chopped green bell pepper
- 14 ounce of diced tomatoes
- 1/2 cup of chopped white onion
- 1 teaspoon of minced garlic
- 1/2 teaspoon of salt
- 1 teaspoon of red chili powder
- 1 teaspoon of ground cumin
- 4-ounce of tomato puree
- 8 fluid ounce of water

Directions:

1. Grease a 6-quarts slow cooker with a non-stick cooking spray and add all the ingredients into it.
2. Stir properly and cover the top.
3. Plug in the slow cooker; adjust the cooking time to 5 hours and let it cook on the high heat setting or until the rice absorbs all the liquid.
4. Serve right away.

Nutrition Value:
Calories:210 Cal, Carbohydrates:11g, Protein:12g, Fats:10g, Fiber:3g.

2. Exquisite Banana, Apple, and Coconut Curry

Yield: 6
Total time: 6 hours and 10 minutes
Ingredients:

- 1/2 cup of amaranth seeds
- 1 apple, cored and sliced
- 1 banana, sliced
- 1 1/2 cups of diced tomatoes
- 3 teaspoons of chopped parsley
- 1 green pepper, chopped
- 1 large white onion, peeled and diced
- 2 teaspoons of minced garlic
- 1 teaspoon of salt
- 1 teaspoon of ground cumin
- 2 1/2 tablespoons of curry powder
- 2 tablespoons of flour
- 2 bay leaves
- 1/2 cup of white wine
- 8 fluid ounce of coconut milk
- 1/2 cup of water

Directions:

1. Using a food processor place the apple, tomatoes, garlic and pulse it until it gets smooth but a little bit chunky.
2. Add this mixture to a 6-quarts slow cooker and add the remaining ingredients.
3. Stir until it mixes properly and cover the top.
4. Plug in the slow cooker; adjust the cooking time to 6 hours and let it cook on the low heat setting or until it is cooked thoroughly.
5. Add the seasoning and serve right away.

Nutrition Value:
Calories:370 Cal, Carbohydrates:15g, Protein:5g, Fats:8g, Fiber:8g.

3. Hearty Vegetarian Lasagna Soup

Yield: 10
Total time: 7 hours and 20 minutes
Ingredients:

- 12 ounces of lasagna noodles
- 4 cups of spinach leaves
- 2 cups of brown mushrooms, sliced
- 2 medium-sized zucchinis, stemmed and sliced
- 28 ounce of crushed tomatoes
- 1 medium-sized white onion, peeled and diced
- 2 teaspoon of minced garlic
- 1 tablespoon of dried basil
- 2 bay leaves
- 2 teaspoons of salt
- 1/8 teaspoon of red pepper flakes
- 2 teaspoons of ground black pepper
- 2 teaspoons of dried oregano
- 15-ounce of tomato sauce
- 6 cups of vegetable broth

Directions:

1. Grease a 6-quarts slow cooker and place all the ingredients in it except for the lasagna and spinach.
2. Cover the top, plug in the slow cooker; adjust the cooking time to 7 hours and let it cook on the low heat setting or until it is properly done.
3. In the meantime, cook the lasagna noodles in the boiling water for 7 to 10 minutes or until it gets soft.
4. Then drain and set it aside until the slow cooker is done cooking.
5. When it is done, add the lasagna noodles into the soup along with the spinach and continue cooking for 10 to 15 minutes or until the spinach leaves wilts.
6. Using a ladle, serving it in a bowl.

Nutrition Value:
Calories:188 Cal, Carbohydrates:13g, Protein:18g, Fats:9g, Fiber:0g.

4. Tastiest Barbecued Tofu and Vegetables

Yield: 4
Total time: 4 hours 15 minutes
Ingredients:

- 14-ounce of extra-firm tofu, pressed and drained
- 2 medium-sized zucchini, stemmed and diced
- 1/2 large green bell pepper, cored and cubed
- 3 stalks of broccoli stalks
- 8 ounce of sliced water chestnuts
- 1 small white onion, peeled and minced
- 1 1/2 teaspoon of minced garlic
- 2 teaspoons of minced ginger
- 1 1/2 teaspoon of salt
- 1/8 teaspoon of ground black pepper
- 1/4 teaspoon of crushed red pepper
- 1/4 teaspoon of five spice powder
- 2 teaspoons of molasses
- 1 tablespoon of whole-grain mustard
- 1/4 teaspoon of vegan Worcestershire sauce
- 8 ounces of tomato sauce
- 1/4 cup of hoisin sauce
- 1 tablespoon of soy sauce
- 2 tablespoons of apple cider vinegar
- 2 tablespoons of water

Directions:

1. Take a 6-quarts slow cooker, grease it with a non-stick cooking spray and set it aside until it is required.
2. Place a medium-sized non-stick skillet pan over an average heat, add the oil and let it heat.
3. Cut the tofu into 1/2 inch pieces and add it to the skillet pan in a single layer.
4. Cook for 3 minutes per sides and then transfer it to the prepared slow cooker.
5. When the tofu turns brown, place it into the pan, add the onion, garlic, ginger and cook for 3 to 5 minutes or until the onions are softened.

6. Add the remaining ingredients into the pan except for the vegetables which are the broccoli stalks, zucchini, bell pepper and water chestnuts.
7. Stir until it mixes properly and cook for 2 minutes or until the mixture starts bubbling.
8. Transfer this mixture into the slow cooker and stir properly.
9. Cover the top, plug in the slow cooker; adjust the cooking time to 3 hours and let it cook on the high heat setting or until it is cooked thoroughly.
10. In the meantime, trim the broccoli stalks and cut it into 1/4 inch pieces.
11. When the tofu is cooked thoroughly, put it into the slow cooker; add the broccoli stalks and the remaining vegetables.
12. Stir until it mixes properly and then return the top to cover it.
13. Continue cooking for 1 hour at the high heat setting or until the vegetables are tender.
14. Serve right away with rice.

Nutrition Value:
Calories:189 Cal, Carbohydrates:19g, Protein:12g, Fats:9g, Fiber:3g.

5. Inexpensive Bean and Spinach Enchiladas

Yield: 8
Total time: 3 hours
Ingredients:

- 2 cups of cooked black beans
- 1 cup of frozen corn
- 10 ounce of chopped spinach
- Half of a medium-sized cucumber, peeled and sliced
- 6 cups of chopped lettuce
- 4 medium-sized radishes, peeled and cut into matchsticks
- 1/2 cup of cherry tomatoes, halved
- 1 teaspoon of salt, divided
- 1/2 teaspoon of ground black pepper, divided
- 1/2 teaspoon of ground cumin
- 3 1/2 cups of tomato salsa
- 2 cups of grated vegetarian cheddar cheese
- 8 corn tortillas, about 6-inch
- 3 tablespoons lime juice
- 2 tablespoons olive oil

Directions:

1. Place 1 cup of beans in a medium-sized bowl then ,using a fork mash them.
2. Then add the remaining beans, corn, spinach, 1/2 teaspoon of salt, 1/4 teaspoon of black pepper, 1 cup of cheddar cheese and stir until it mixes well.
3. Take a 6-quarts slow cooker and spread 2 cups of tomato salsa on the bottom.
4. Place the tortillas on a clean working space and proportionally top it with the prepared bean mixture, at least 1/2 cup.
5. Roll up the tortillas and place it into the slow cooker on top of the salsa, seam-side down.
6. Top it with the remaining tomato salsa, cheese and cover the top.
7. Plug in the slow cooker; adjust the cooking time to 3 hours and let it cook on the the low heat setting or until the cheese melts completely.
8. In the meantime, using a bowl, place the cucumber, lettuce, radish and tomatoes in it, sprinkle it with the lime juice, oil, the remaining of each salt and black pepper.
9. Toss to cover and serve this with the cooked enchiladas.

Nutrition Value:
Calories:239 Cal, Carbohydrates:31g, Protein:16g, Fats:8.5g, Fiber:9g.

6. Delightful Coconut Vegetarian Curry

Yield: 6
Total time: 4 hours and 20 minutes
Ingredients:

- 5 medium-sized potatoes, peeled and cut into 1-inch cubes
- 1/4 cup of curry powder
- 2 tablespoons of flour
- 1 tablespoon of chili powder
- 1/2 teaspoon of red pepper flakes
- 1/2 teaspoon of cayenne pepper
- 1 large green bell pepper, cut into strips
- 1 large red bell pepper, cut into strips
- 2 tablespoons of onion soup mix
- 14-ounce of coconut cream, unsweetened
- 3 cups of vegetable broth
- 2 medium-sized carrots, peeled and cut into matchstick
- 1 cup of green peas
- 1/4 cup of chopped cilantro

Directions:

1. Take a 6-quarts slow cooker, grease it with a non-stick cooking spray and place the potatoes pieces in the bottom.
2. Add the remaining ingredients except for the carrots, peas and cilantro.
3. Stir properly and cover the top.
4. Plug in the slow cooker; adjust the cooking time to 4 hours and let it cook on the low heat setting or until it cooks thoroughly.
5. When the cooking time is over, add the carrots to the curry and continue cooking for 30 minutes.
6. Then, add the peas and continue cooking for another 30 minutes or until the peas get tender.
7. Garnish it with cilantro and serve.

Nutrition Value:
Calories:369 Cal, Carbohydrates:39g, Protein:7g, Fats:23g, Fiber:8g.

7. Super tasty Vegetarian Chili

Yield: 6
Total time: 2 hours and 10 minutes
Ingredients:

- 16-ounce of vegetarian baked beans
- 16 ounce of cooked chickpeas
- 16 ounce of cooked kidney beans
- 15 ounce of cooked corn
- 1 medium-sized green bell pepper, cored and chopped
- 2 stalks of celery, peeled and chopped
- 12 ounce of chopped tomatoes
- 1 medium-sized white onion, peeled and chopped
- 1 teaspoon of minced garlic
- 1 teaspoon of salt
- 1 tablespoon of red chili powder
- 1 tablespoon of dried oregano
- 1 tablespoon of dried basil
- 1 tablespoon of dried parsley
- 18-ounce of black bean soup
- 4-ounce of tomato puree

Directions:

1. Take a 6-quarts slow cooker, grease it with a non-stick cooking spray and place all the ingredients into it.
2. Stir properly and cover the top.
3. Plug in the slow cooker; adjust the cooking time to 2 hours and let it cook on the high heat setting or until it is cooked thoroughly.
4. Serve right away.

Nutrition Value:
Calories:190 Cal, Carbohydrates:35g, Protein:11g, Fats:1g, Fiber:10g.

8. Vegetable Soup

Yield: 8
Total time: 6 hours and 30 minutes
Ingredients:

- 1/4 cup of vegetable shortening
- 2 cups of all-purpose flour, leveled
- 1/2 cup of barley, uncooked
- 16 ounce of diced tomatoes
- 2 medium-sized potatoes, peeled and cubed
- 16 ounce of frozen mixed vegetables
- 1 large white onion, peeled and diced
- 1 1/2 teaspoon of minced garlic
- 6 cups of vegetable broth
- 1/2 teaspoon of salt
- 1/2 teaspoon of dried basil
- 1/2 teaspoon of ground black pepper
- 1 teaspoon of dried oregano
- 1 teaspoon of dried parsley
- 1 bay leaf
- 6 1/4 cup of vegetable broth

Directions:

1. Take a 6 quarts slow cooker, grease it with a non-stick cooking spray and add all the ingredients except for flour, vegetable shortening and reserve 1/4 cup of vegetable broth.
2. Stir properly and cover the top.
3. Plug in the slow cooker; adjust the cooking time to 6 hours and let it cook on the low heat setting or until it is cooked thoroughly.
4. In the meantime, place the flour, shortening in a food processor and pulse it until the mixture resembles crumbs.
5. Then gradually mix the reserved 1/4 cup of vegetable broth until the smooth dough comes together.
6. Transfer the dough to a clean space filled with flour and roll it into the 1/8 thick dough.
7. Using a sharp knife cut the dough into small squares and put them in the slow cooker when 6 hours of cooking time is over.
8. Continue cooking for 1 hour at the high heat setting or until the dumplings are soft.
9. Scoop it into the serving bowls and serve.

Nutrition Value:
Calories:218 Cal, Carbohydrates:31g, Protein:7g, Fats:8g, Fiber:6g.

9. Creamy Sweet Potato & Coconut Curry

Yield: 6
Total time: 6 hours and 20 minutes
Ingredients:

- 2 pounds of sweet potatoes, peeled and chopped
- 1/2 pound of red cabbage, shredded
- 2 red chilies, seeded and sliced
- 2 medium-sized red bell peppers, cored and sliced
- 2 large white onions, peeled and sliced
- 1 1/2 teaspoon of minced garlic
- 1 teaspoon of grated ginger
- 1/2 teaspoon of salt
- 1 teaspoon of paprika
- 1/2 teaspoon of cayenne pepper
- 2 tablespoons of peanut butter
- 4 tablespoons of olive oil
- 12-ounce of tomato puree
- 14 fluid ounce of coconut milk
- 1/2 cup of chopped coriander

Directions:

1. Place a large non-stick skillet pan over an average heat, add 1 tablespoon of oil and let it heat.
2. Then add the onion and cook for 10 minutes or until it gets soft.
3. Add the garlic, ginger, salt, paprika, cayenne pepper and continue cooking for 2 minutes or until it starts producing fragrance.
4. Transfer this mixture to a 6-quarts slow cooker, and reserve the pan.
5. In the pan, add 1 tablespoon of oil and let it heat.
6. Add the cabbage, red chili, bell pepper and cook it for 5 minutes.
7. Then transfer this mixture to the slow cooker and reserve the pan.
8. Add the remaining oil to the pan; the sweet potatoes in a single layer and cook it in 3 batches for 5 minutes or until it starts getting brown.
9. Add the sweet potatoes to the slow cooker, along with tomato puree, coconut milk and stir properly.
10. Cover the top, plug in the slow cooker; adjust the cooking time to 6 hours and let it cook on the low heat setting or until the sweet potatoes are tender.
11. When done, add the seasoning and pour it in the peanut butter.
12. Garnish it with coriander and serve.

Nutrition Value:
Calories:434 Cal, Carbohydrates:47g, Protein:6g, Fats:22g, Fiber:3g.

10. Comforting Chickpea Tagine

Yield: 6
Total time: 4 hours and 15 minutes
Ingredients:

- 14 ounce of cooked chickpeas
- 12 dried apricots
- 1 red bell pepper, cored and sliced
- 1 small butternut squash, peeled, cored and chopped
- 2 zucchini, stemmed and chopped
- 1 medium-sized white onion, peeled and chopped
- 1 teaspoon of minced garlic
- 1 teaspoon of ground ginger
- 1 1/2 teaspoon of salt
- 1 teaspoon of ground black pepper
- 1 teaspoon of ground cumin
- 2 teaspoon of paprika
- 1 teaspoon of harissa paste
- 2 teaspoon of honey
- 2 tablespoons of olive oil
- 1 pound of passata
- 1/4 cup of chopped coriander

Directions:

1. Take a 6-quarts slow cooker, grease it with a non-stick cooking spray and place the chickpeas, apricots, bell pepper, butternut squash, zucchini and onion into it.
2. Sprinkle it with salt, black pepper and set it aside until it is called for.
3. Place a large non-stick skillet pan over an average temperature of heat; add the oil, garlic, cumin and paprika.
4. Stir properly and cook for 1 minutes or until it starts producing fragrance.
5. Then pour in the harissa paste, honey, passata and boil the mixture.
6. When the mixture is done boiling, pour this mixture over the vegetables in the slow cooker and cover it with the lid.
7. Plug in the slow cooker; adjust the cooking time to 4 hours and let it cook on the high heat setting or until the vegetables gets tender.
8. When done, add the seasoning, garnish it with the coriander and serve right away.

Nutrition Value:
Calories:237 Cal, Carbohydrates:45g, Protein:9g, Fats:2g, Fiber:8g.

NICE SIDE DISHES

1. Creamy Creamed Corn

Yield: 5
Total time: 4 hours
Ingredients:

- 16 ounce of frozen corn kernels
- 1 teaspoon of salt and
- 1/2 teaspoon of ground black pepper
- 1 tablespoon honey
- 1/2 cup of vegetarian butter, unsalted
- 8-ounce of cream cheese, softened
- 1/2 cup of almond milk

Directions:

1. Take a 6-quarts slow cooker, grease it with a non-stick cooking spray and place ingredients in it.
2. Stir properly and cover the top.
3. Plug in the slow cooker; adjust the cooking time to 4 hours and let it cook on the low heat setting or until it is cooked thoroughly.
4. Serve right away.

Nutrition Value:
Calories:120 Cal, Carbohydrates:28g, Protein:2g, Fats:1g, Fiber:4g.

2. *Savory Squash & Apple Dish*

Yield: 6
Total time: 4 hours and 15 minutes
Ingredients:

- 8 ounce of dried cranberries
- 4 medium-sized apples, peeled, cored and chopped
- 3 pounds of butternut squash, peeled, seeded and cubed
- Half of a medium-sized white onion, peeled and diced
- 1 tablespoon of ground cinnamon
- 1 1/2 teaspoons of ground nutmeg

Directions:

1. Take a 6-quarts slow cooker, grease it with a non-stick cooking spray and place the ingredients in it.
2. Stir properly and cover the top.
3. Plug in the slow cooker; adjust the cooking time to 4 hours and let it cook on the low heat setting or until it cooks thoroughly.
4. Serve right away.

Nutrition Value:
Calories:210 Cal, Carbohydrates:11g, Protein:3g, Fats:5g, Fiber:6g.

3. Spicy Cajun Boiled Peanuts

Yield: 15
Total time: 8 hours and 5 minutes
Ingredients:

- 5 pounds of peanuts, raw and in shells
- 6-ounce of dry crab boil
- 4-ounce of jalapeno peppers, sliced
- 2-ounce of vegetable broth

Directions:

1. Take a 6-quarts slow cooker place the ingredients in it and cover it with water.
2. Stir properly and cover the top.
3. Plug in the slow cooker; adjust the cooking time to 8 hours and let it cook on the low heat setting or until the peanuts are soft and floats on top of the cooking liquid.
4. Drain the nuts and serve right away.

Nutrition Value:
Calories:309 Cal, Carbohydrates:5g, Protein:0g, Fats:26g, Fiber:0g.

4. Wonderful Steamed Artichoke

Yield: 4
Total time: 4 hours and 5 minutes
Ingredients:

- 8 medium-sized artichokes, stemmed and trimmed
- 2 teaspoons of salt
- 4 tablespoons of lemon juice

Directions:

1. Cut 1-inch part of the artichoke from the top and place it in a 6-quarts slow cooker, facing an upright position.
2. Using a bowl, place the lemon juice and pour in the salt until it mixes properly.
3. Pour this mixture over the artichoke and add the water to cover at least ¾ of the artichokes.
4. Cover the top, plug in the slow cooker; adjust the cooking time to 4 hours and let it cook on the high heat setting or until the artichokes get soft.
5. Serve immediately.

Nutrition Value:
Calories:78 Cal, Carbohydrates:17g, Protein:5g, Fats: 0g, Fiber:9g.

5. Creamy Garlic Cauliflower Mashed Potatoes

Yield: 6
Total time: 3 hours
Ingredients:

- 30-ounce of cauliflower head, cut into florets
- 6 garlic cloves, peeled
- 1 teaspoon of salt
- 3/4 teaspoon of ground black pepper
- 1 bay leaf
- 1 tablespoon of vegetarian butter, unsalted
- 3 cups of water

Directions:

1. Take a 6-quarts slow cooker, grease it with a non-stick cooking spray and place the cauliflower florets into it.
2. Add the remaining ingredients except for the butter and stir properly.
3. Cover the top, plug in the slow cooker; adjust the cooking time to 3 hours and let it cook on the high heat setting or until it is cooked thoroughly.
4. When done, open the slow cooker, remove the bay leaf and garlic cloves.
5. Drain the cooking liquid, add the butter and let it melt.
6. Then using an immersion blender, mash the cauliflower or until it gets creamy.
7. Add the seasoning and serve.

Nutrition Value:
Calories:66 Cal, Carbohydrates:6g, Protein:3g, Fats:4.2g, Fiber:3g.

6. Healthy Pumpkin Risotto

Yield: 4
Total time: 1 hour and 45 minutes
Ingredients:

- 2 tablespoons of olive oil
- 1/2 cup of chopped white onion
- 1 tablespoon of minced garlic
- 2 teaspoons of salt
- 1 teaspoon of ground black pepper
- 2 teaspoons of dried sage
- 1 1/2 cups of short grain rice
- 2 cups of roasted pumpkin
- 32 fluid ounce vegetable broth

Directions:

1. Place a medium-sized non-stick skillet pan over an average temperature of heat, add and let it heat.
2. Then add the onion, garlic, sage and heat it for 5 minutes or until it gets softened.
3. Pour in the rice and continue cooking for 3 minutes.
4. Transfer this mixture to a 6-quarts slow cooker and add the remaining ingredients except for pumpkin seeds.
5. Stir properly and cover the top.
6. Plug in the slow cooker; adjust the cooking time to 1 hour 30 minutes and let it cook on the high heat setting or until the rice gets soft.
7. Serve right away.

Nutrition Value:
Calories:190 Cal, Carbohydrates:11g, Protein:12g, Fats:10g, Fiber:3g.

7. Flavorful Roasted Peppers

Yield: 5
Total time: 3 hours and 20 minutes
Ingredients:

- 5 medium-sized red bell pepper, cored and halved

Directions:

1. Take a 6-quarts slow cooker, grease it with a non-stick cooking spray and add the peppers.
2. Cover the top, plug in the slow cooker; adjust the cooking time to 3 hours and let it cook on the high heat setting or until the peppers are softened, stirring halfway through.
3. When done, remove the peppers from the cooker and let it cool off completely.
4. Then remove the pepper peels by tugging it from the edge or with a paring knife.
5. Serve as desired.

Nutrition Value:
Calories:5 Cal, Carbohydrates:1g, Protein:0g, Fats:0g, Fiber:0g.

8. Comforting Spinach and Artichoke Dip

Yield: 8
Total time: 2 hours and 25 minutes
Ingredients:

- 8-ounce of frozen spinach, thawed and squeezed
- 8 ounce of diced water chestnuts
- 28 ounce of cooked artichoke hearts, chopped
- 1 teaspoon of minced garlic
- 1 teaspoon of salt
- 3/4 teaspoon of ground black pepper
- 2 tablespoons of nutritional yeast
- 1 cup of cashew, raw
- 2 teaspoons of whole-grain mustard paste
- 2 tablespoons of lemon juice
- 3 tablespoons of soy-mayonnaise
- 1 cup of almond milk, unsweetened

Directions:

1. Using a food processor, place the cashews and pulse it until the mixture looks like flour, while ensuring not to over-blend.
2. Add the garlic, salt, mustard paste, lemon juice, almond milk and mash it for 2 minutes or until it gets smooth.
3. Place this mixture into a 6-quarts slow cooker, add the remaining ingredients except for the mayonnaise and stir properly.
4. Cover the top, plug in the slow cooker; adjust the cooking time to 4 hours and let it cook on the high heat setting.
5. When done, open the slow cooker and pour in and stir the mayonnaise properly.
6. Add thr seasoning and serve.

Nutrition Value:
Calories:83 Cal, Carbohydrates:16g, Protein:4g, Fats:0g, Fiber:5g.

9. Healthy Coconut Basil Tofu

Yield: 5
Total time: 4 hours and 5 minutes
Ingredients:

- 12-ounce of firm tofu, pressed and drained
- 4 cups of baby bok choy, rinsed
- 8-ounce of mushrooms, sliced
- 1 medium-sized white onion, peeled and sliced
- 1 teaspoon of minced garlic
- 1 1/2 tablespoon of grated ginger
- 1 teaspoon of salt
- 1 tablespoon of coconut sugar
- 1/2 teaspoon of crushed red pepper flakes
- 1/4 cup of cornstarch
- 3/4 cup of chopped basil
- 2 tablespoon of tamari sauce
- 2 tablespoons of apple cider vinegar
- 1 tablespoon of fish sauce
- 1 cup of vegetable broth
- 14-ounce of coconut milk, unsweetened

Directions:

1. Cut the tofu into large strips, halve bok choy, onion and cut it into large chunks.
2. Using a bowl pour in and stir the ginger, basil, vinegar, tamari sauce, vinegar, fish sauce and the vegetable broth.
3. Pour this mixture into a 6-quarts slow cooker and add the remaining ingredients except for the cornstarch.
4. Toss to cover and then cover the top.
5. Plug in the slow cooker; adjust the cooking time to 3 hours 30 minutes and let it cook on the high heat setting.
6. Then stir in the cornstarch and continue cooking for another 30 minutes.
7. Add the seasoning and serve.

Nutrition Value:
Calories:20 Cal, Carbohydrates:2g, Protein:3g, Fats:0.5g, Fiber:0.3g.

10. Amazing Brussels Sprouts

Yield: 6
Total time: 4 hours and 20 minutes
Ingredients:

- 2 pounds of Brussels sprouts, trimmed and halved
- 1 1/2 teaspoon of salt
- 1 teaspoon of ground black pepper
- 2 tablespoons of brown sugar
- 2 tablespoons of unsalted vegan butter, grated
- 1/2 cup of apple cider vinegar
- 2 tablespoons of olive oil
- 1/4 cup of grated vegetarian Parmesan cheese

Directions:

1. Place a small saucepan over an average temperature of heat, add the vinegar, suga,r stir and boil the mixture.
2. Switch the heat to a medium-low and let it cook for 6 to 8 minutes or until the sauce reduces by half, thereafter let it cool off completely.
3. Place the Brussels sprouts in a 4-quarts slow cooker, add the salt, black pepper, oil and then top it with the butter.
4. Cover the top, plug in the slow cooker; adjust the cooking time to 2 hours and let it cook on the high heat setting.
5. When done, sprinkle it with the prepared vinegar sauce and toss it to coat.
6. Garnish it with cheese and serve.

Nutrition Value:
Calories:46 Cal, Carbohydrates:10g, Protein:3.2g, Fats:0.3g, Fiber:3.5g.

SUPER BREAD AND DESSERTS

1. Sumptuous Blueberry Lemon Cake

Yield: 6
Total time: 4 hours and 15 minutes
Ingredients:

- 1/4 cup of blueberries, fresh
- 1/2 cup of whole-wheat pastry flour
- 1 teaspoon of ground flaxseeds
- 1/4 teaspoon of stevia
- 1/4 teaspoon of baking powder
- 1/2 teaspoon of lemon zest
- 1 teaspoon of maple syrup
- 1/4 teaspoon of vanilla extract, unsweetened
- 1/4 teaspoon of lemon extract
- 1 teaspoon of olive oil
- 2 teaspoons of water, warmed
- 1/3 cup of almond milk, unsweetened

Directions:

1. Using a small bowl, stir the flax seeds and let sit for 10 minutes.
2. In the meantime, grease a 6-quarts slow cooker with a non-stick cooking spray and then line with a parchment sheet.
3. In a large bowl place flour and mix in stevia and baking powder.
4. In another bowl stir together remaining ingredients along with flax seeds mixture until combined and then gradually stir into prepared flour mixture until incorporated.
5. Spoon this batter into the prepared slow cooker and smooth the top with a spatula.
6. Cover with top wrapped with a paper towel and plug in the slow cooker.
7. Adjust cooking time to 1 hour and 20 minutes and let cook on high heat setting or until an inserted wooden skewer into the center of the cake comes out clean.
8. Pull out cake using parchment sheet and let cool on wire rack.
9. Slice to serve.

Nutrition Value:
Calories:369 Cal, Carbohydrates:56g, Protein:5g, Fats:15g, Fiber:5g.

2. *Heavenly Chocolate Peanut Butter Cake*

Yield: 8
Total time: 3 hours
Ingredients:

- 1 cup of plain flour, leveled
- 1/4 cup of and 3 tablespoons cocoa powder, unsweetened
- 1 1/2 teaspoon of baking powder
- 1 1/4 cup of brown sugar, divided
- 1 teaspoon of vanilla extract, unsweetened
- 1/2 cup of peanut butter
- 2 tablespoons of vegan margarine, melted
- 4 fluid ounce of soy milk
- 2 cups of boiling water

Directions:

1. Place the flour in a large bowl, add the baking powder, 3 tablespoons of cocoa powder, along with 1/2 cup of sugar and stir properly.
2. Pour in the milk, vanilla, margarine and whisk evenly.
3. Take a 4-quarts slow cooker, grease it with a non-stick cooking spray and add the prepared flour mixture.
4. Using a separate dish, mix the remaining cocoa powder and sugar.
5. Then in a separate bowl, place the peanut butter, using an immersive blender, blend it with water until it gets smooth.
6. Blend in the cocoa-sugar mixture properly and then pour this mixture into the slow cooker over the flour batter.
7. Cover the top, plug in the slow cooker; adjust the cooking time to 2 hours and let it cook on the high heat setting or until an inserted wooden skewer into the center of the cake comes out clean.
8. When done, turn out the cake, let it cool off over the wire rack completely and slice to serve.

Nutrition Value:
Calories:437 Cal, Carbohydrates:59g, Protein:6g, Fats:21g, Fiber:1g.

3. Fudgy Chocolate Pudding Cake

Yield: 8
Total time: 3 hours
Ingredients:

- 1 cup of all-purpose flour, leveled
- 1 1/4 cup of coconut sugar
- 1/4 cup and 2 tablespoons of cocoa powder, unsweetened
- 1/2 teaspoon of salt
- 2 teaspoons of baking powder
- 1 teaspoon of vanilla extract, unsweetened
- 2 tablespoons of olive oil
- 4 fluid ounce of chocolate almond milk
- 1 1/2 cups of hot water

Directions:

1. Using a medium-sized bowl place the flour, add the salt, 1/2 cup of sugar, baking powder, 2 tablespoons of cocoa powder and stir properly.
2. Whisk the vanilla, oil and the milk until the smooth batter comes together.
3. Take a 4 quarts slow cooker and grease it with a non-stick cooking spray.
4. Scoop the prepared cake batter into the prepared slow cooker and smoothen the top using a spatula.
5. Using a separate bowl stir the remaining sugar, cocoa powder and then whisk it in the water until it gets smooth.
6. Pour this mixture over cake batter and cover the top.
7. Plug in the slow cooker; adjust the cooking time to 2 hours and let it cook on the high heat setting or until an inserted wooden skewer into the center of the cake comes out clean.
8. When done, let the cake stand for 45 minutes or until it cools off completely, then scoop it out and serve.

Nutrition Value:
Calories:250 Cal, Carbohydrates:49g, Protein:2g, Fats:5g, Fiber:2g.

4. Super Tea Spiced Poached Pears

Yield: 4
Total time: 4 hours and 5 minutes
Ingredients:

- 4 medium-sized pears, peeled
- 1 tablespoon of grated ginger
- 5 cardamom pods
- 1 cinnamon stick, split in half
- 1/4 cup of maple syrup
- 16 fluid ounce of orange juice

Directions:

1. Cut off the bottom of each pear and centralize it.
2. Using a 4 quarts slow cooker, place the pears in an upright position and add the remaining ingredients.
3. Cover the top, plug in the slow cooker; adjust the cooking time to 4 hours and let it cook on the high heat setting or until it gets soft.
4. Sprinkle it with the ground cinnamon over each pear, top it with the nuts and serve.

Nutrition Value:

Calories:98 Cal, Carbohydrates:26g, Protein:1g, Fats: 0g, Fiber:1.5g.

5. Warming Baked Apples

Yield: 5
Total time: 2 hours and 10 minutes
Ingredients:

- 4 medium-sized apples
- 1/2 cup of granola
- 4 teaspoon of maple syrup
- 2 tablespoons of melted vegan butter, unsalted

Directions:

1. Cut off the top of the apple and remove the core from each apple using a measuring spoon.
2. Fill the center of each apple with 1/8 cup of granola and place it in a 4-quarts slow cooker.
3. Drizzle with butter and then sprinkle with a teaspoon maple syrup over each apple.
4. Cover the top, plug in the slow cooker; adjust the cooking time to 2 hours and let it cook on the high heat setting or until it gets tender.
5. Serve right away.

Nutrition Value:
Calories:162 Cal, Carbohydrates:42g, Protein:0.5g, Fats:0.3g, Fiber:4g.

6. Fluffy Whole Wheat Potato Rolls

Yield: 8
Total time: 2 hours and 15 minutes
Ingredients:

- 3 cups of whole wheat flour
- 3/4 cup of mashed potatoes
- 1 teaspoon of salt
- 1 teaspoon of coconut sugar
- 1 teaspoon of nutritional yeast
- 2 tablespoons of olive oil
- 2 tablespoons of chickpeas liquid
- 1/2 cup of vegetable broth

Directions:

1. Using a large bowl place the mashed potatoes, sugar, yeast, vegetable broth and stir well using an immersion blender until it gets smooth.
2. Let the potato mixer rest for 10 minutes or until the mixture rises.
3. Then add and blend the salt, olive oil, chickpea liquid, flour, 1/2 cup at a time until it mixes properly.
4. Transfer dough to a clean surface dusted with flour and knead for 7 to 10 minutes or until smooth dough comes together; knead in more dough if the dough is too wet.
5. Take a 4-quarts slow cooker, line it with a parchment sheet.
6. Evenly divide the dough into 8 pieces and then roll them into balls.
7. Place these balls into the prepared slow cooker, cover the top and wrap it with a dish towel or paper towels.
8. Plug in the slow cooker; adjust the cooking time to 45 minutes and let it cook on the low heat setting or until the rolls rise.
9. Then cook it for 1 hour at the high heat setting.
10. Let the rolls cool off for 15 minutes before serving.

Nutrition Value:
Calories:210 Cal, Carbohydrates:11g, Protein:12g, Fats:10g, Fiber:3g.

7. Pillowy Sandwich Bread

Yield: 8
Total time: 2 hours and 30 minutes
Ingredients:

- 2 cups of all-purpose flour, leveled
- 1 teaspoon of nutritional yeast
- 1 tablespoon of vegan butter, melted
- 1/2 tablespoon of salt
- 1 tablespoons of coconut sugar
- 1/2 cup of coconut milk, unsweetened
- 1/2 cup of warm water

Directions:

1. Place the water in a large bowl, add the yeast, stir properly and let it sit for 5 minutes.
2. Then add the salt, sugar, butter, milk and stir until it mixes properly.
3. Pour in and stir the flour, 1/2 cup at a time, until the moist and sticky dough comes together.
4. Transfer the dough to a clean working space dusted with flour, and kneads for 7 to 10 minutes or until the dough gets smooth and elastic.
5. Shape the dough into a loaf.
6. Take a 4 quarts slow cooker, line it with parchment sheet and place the dough in it.
7. Cover the top with a wrapped dish towel or paper towels, then plug in the slow cooker; adjust the cooking time to 2 hours 30 minutes and let it cook on the high heat setting.
8. Check the loaf firstly when 1 hour of cooking time is over, when 30 minutes of the cooking time is over and then at a 15 minutes intervals.
9. The loaf will be done if an inserted wooden skewer into the loaf comes out clean.
10. Transfer the loaf into a preheated broiler, broil for 5 minutes or until the top are nicely browned and crusty.
11. Let the loaf cool on the wire rack before slicing to serve.

Nutrition Value:
Calories:93 Cal, Carbohydrates:18g, Protein:3g, Fats:1g, Fiber:0g.

8. Chewy Olive Parmesan Bread

Yield: 8
Total time: 4 hours
Ingredients:

- 3 cups of bread flour, leveled
- 3/4 cup of diced olives
- 1/2 tablespoon of minced garlic
- 1 teaspoon of nutritional yeast
- 1/4 cup of grated vegetarian Parmesan cheese
- 1 1/2 cups of water

Directions:

1. Using a large bowl, place the flour and add the remaining ingredients except for water.
2. Stir properly, add some water and stir again until the moist dough comes together.
3. Cover the bowl with a damp towel and let it sit for 1 1/2 hours in a warm place or until the dough expands double in size.
4. Then take a large parchment sheet, sprinkle it with flour and place the dough on it.
5. Shape the dough along with parchment sheet into round balls, cover it with a plastic wrap and let it sit for another 30 minutes.
6. Plug in the slow cooker and let cook at the high heat setting.
7. Drop the dough wrapped in the parchment sheet into the slow cooker and tuck to fit into it properly.
8. Cover the top with a wrapped dish towel or parchment sheets and let it cook for 2 hours at the high heat setting or until an inserted wooden skewer into the loaf comes out clean.
9. Transfer the loaf into a preheated oven at 400 degrees F and bake for 15 to 20 minutes or until the top is nicely browned and crusty.
10. Let the loaf cool off on a wire rack before slicing to serve.

Nutrition Value:
Calories:110 Cal, Carbohydrates:14g, Protein: 2g, Fats:6g, Fiber:0g.

9. Crusty Rosemary Bread

Yield: 8
Total time: 3 hours and 50 minutes
Ingredients:

- 10-ounce of all-purpose flour, leveled
- 1 teaspoon of nutritional yeast
- 1 1/2 teaspoons of salt
- 2 tablespoons of chopped rosemary, and more for sprinkling
- 2 tablespoons of olive oil, and more for brushing
- 1 cup of water, lukewarm

Directions:

1. Using a large bowl, place the flour and add the remaining ingredients except for water.
2. Stir properly, add 3/4 cup of water and stir again until the moist dough comes together, add more water if need be.
3. Cover the bowl with a damp towel and let it sit for 30 minutes in a warm place.
4. Then knead the dough for 3 minutes, return it to the bowl, cover it with a damp cloth and let it sit for another 30 minutes in a warm place.
5. Massage the dough again for 3 minutes, return it to the bowl, cover it with a damp cloth and let it sit for another 2 to 3 hours in a warm place or until the dough expands double in size.
6. Transfers the dough to a clean working space covered with flour, and mold it into balls.
7. Then take a large parchment sheet, sprinkle it with flour and place the dough on it.
8. Brush the top of the dough with olive oil, sprinkle it with rosemary leaves and lower it into a 6-quarts slow cooker.
9. Cover the top and let the dough rest for 1 hour.
10. Then plug in the slow cooker and let it cook at the high heat setting for 2 hours or until an inserted wooden skewer into the loaf comes out clean, while checking the dough at a 45 minutes intervals.
11. Transfer the loaf into a preheated broiler and broil it for 5 minutes or until the top are nicely browned and crusty.
12. Let the loaf cool off on the wire rack before slicing to serve.

Nutrition Value:
Calories:190 Cal, Carbohydrates:19g, Protein:5g, Fats:11g, Fiber:1g.

10. Rich Cornbread

Yield: 6
Total time: 1 hour and 30 minutes
Ingredients:

- 1 cup of all-purpose flour, leveled
- 1 cup of cornmeal
- 1 teaspoon of baking powder
- 1/2 teaspoon of salt
- 2 tablespoons of coconut sugar
- 1/2 teaspoon of baking soda
- 1 1/2 tablespoons of apple cider vinegar
- 2 tablespoons of olive oil
- 12 fluid ounce of soymilk

Directions:

1. Using a large bowl, pour the milk, stir in the vinegar and let it stand for 10 minutes.
2. Then pour in and stir the flour, cornmeal, salt, sugar, baking soda and the baking powder properly.
3. Line a 4-quarts slow cooker with a parchment sheet, scoop the prepared batter into it, and smooth en the top with a spatula.
4. Cover the top with a wrapped dish towel or parchment sheets and let it cook for 1 hour 30 minutes at the high heat setting or until an inserted wooden skewer into the bread comes out clean.
5. When done, pull out the parchment sheet and let the bread cool off on the wire rack.
6. Slice to serve.

Nutrition Value:
Calories:168 Cal, Carbohydrates:21g, Protein:3g, Fats:7g, Fiber:1g.

AMAZING SOUPS & STEWS

1. Bursting Black Bean Soup

Yield: 6
Total time: 8 hours and 10 minutes
Ingredients:

- 1 pound of black beans, uncooked
- 1/4 cup of lentils, uncooked
- 1 medium-sized carrot, peeled and chopped
- 2 medium-sized green bell peppers, cored and chopped
- 1 stalk of celery, chopped
- 28 ounce of diced tomatoes
- 2 jalapeno pepper, seeded and minced
- 1 large red onion, peeled and chopped
- 3 teaspoons of minced garlic
- 1 tablespoon of salt
- 1/2 teaspoon ground black pepper
- 2 tablespoons of red chili powder
- 2 teaspoons of ground cumin
- 1/2 teaspoon of dried oregano
- 3 tablespoons of apple cider vinegar
- 1/2 cup of brown rice, uncooked
- 3 quarts of water, divided

Directions:

1. Place a large pot over medium-high heat, add the beans, pour in 1 1/2 quarts of water and boil it.
2. Let it boil for 10 minutes, then remove the pot from the heat, let it stand for 1 hour and then cover the pot.
3. Drain the beans and add it to a 6-quarts slow cooker.
4. Pour in the remaining 1 1/2 quarts of water and cover it with the lid.
5. Plug in the slow cooker and let it cook for 3 hours at the high setting or until it gets soft.
6. When the beans are done, add the remaining ingredients except for the rice and continue cooking for 3 hours on the low heat setting.
7. When it is30 minutes left to finish, add the rice to the slow cooker and let it cook.
8. When done, using an immersion blender process half of the soup and then serve.

Nutrition Value:
Calories:116 Cal, Carbohydrates:19g, Protein:5.6g, Fats:1.5g, Fiber:4g.

2. *Yummy Lentil Rice Soup*

Yield: 6
Total time: 4 hours and 15 minutes
Ingredients:

- 2 cups of brown rice, uncooked
- 2 cups of lentils, uncooked
- 1/2 cup of chopped celery
- 1 cup of chopped carrots
- 1 cup of sliced mushrooms
- 1/2 of a medium-sized white onion, peeled and chopped
- 1 teaspoon of minced garlic
- 1 tablespoon of salt
- 1/2 teaspoon of ground black pepper
- 1 cup of vegetable broth
- 8 cups of water

Directions:

1. Using a 6-quarts slow cooker, place all the ingredients except for mushrooms and stir until it mixes properly.
2. Cover with lid, plug in the slow cooker and let it cook for 3 to 4 hours at the high setting or until it is cooked thoroughly.
3. Pour in the mushrooms, stir and continue cooking for 1 hour at the low heat setting or until it is done.
4. Serve right away.

Nutrition Value:
Calories:226 Cal, Carbohydrates:41g, Protein:13g, Fats:2g, Fiber:12g.

3. Tangy Corn Chowder

Yield: 6
Total time: 5 hours and 15 minutes
Ingredients:

- 24 ounce of cooked kernel corn
- 3 medium-sized potatoes, peeled and diced
- 2 red chile peppers, minced
- 1 large white onion, peeled and diced
- 1 teaspoon of minced garlic
- 2 teaspoons of salt
- 1/2 teaspoon of ground black pepper
- 1 tablespoon of red chili powder
- 1 tablespoon of dried parsley
- 1/4 cup of vegan margarine
- 14 fluid ounce of soy milk
- 1 lime, juiced
- 24 fluid ounce of vegetable broth

Directions:

1. Using a 6-quarts slow cooker place all the ingredients except for the soy milk, margarine, and lime juice.
2. Stir properly and cover it with the lid.
3. Then plug in the slow cooker and let it cook for 3 to 4 hours at the high setting or until it is cooked thoroughly.
4. When done, process the mixture with an immersion blender or until it gets smooth.
5. Pour in the milk, margarine and stir properly.
6. Continue cooking the soup for 1 hour at the low heat setting.
7. Drizzle it with the lime juice and serve.

Nutrition Value:
Calories:237 Cal, Carbohydrates:18g, Protein:7.4g, Fats:15g, Fiber:2.2g.

4. Healthy Cabbage Soup

Yield: 6
Total time: 4 hours and 15 minutes
Ingredients:

- 5 cups of shredded cabbage
- 3 medium-sized carrots, peeled and chopped
- 3 1/2 cups of diced tomatoes
- 1 medium-sized white onion, chopped
- 2 teaspoons of minced garlic
- 1 teaspoon of salt
- 1 teaspoon of dried oregano
- 1 tablespoon of dried parsley
- 1 1/2 cups of tomato sauce
- 5 cups of vegetable broth

Directions:

1. Using a 6-quarts slow cooker, place all the ingredients and stir properly.
2. Cover it with the lid, plug in the slow cooker and let it cook for 4 hours at the high heat setting or until the vegetables are tender.
3. Serve right away.

Nutrition Value:
Calories:150 Cal, Carbohydrates:4g, Protein:20g, Fats:5g, Fiber:2g.

5. Chunky Potato Soup

Yield: 6
Total time: 6 hours and 10 minutes
Ingredients:

- 1 medium-sized carrot, grated
- 6 medium-sized potatoes, peeled and diced
- 2 stalks of celery, diced
- 1 medium-sized white onion, peeled and diced
- 2 teaspoons of minced garlic
- 1 1/2 teaspoons of salt
- 1 teaspoon of ground black pepper
- 1 1/2 teaspoons of dried sage
- 1 teaspoon of dried thyme
- 2 tablespoons of olive oil
- 2 bay leaves
- 8 1/2 cups of vegetable water

Directions:

1. Using a 6-quarts slow cooker, place all the ingredients and stir properly.
2. Cover it with the lid, plug in the slow cooker and let it cook for 6 hours at the high heat setting or until the potatoes are tender.
3. Serve right away.

Nutrition Value:
Calories:200 Cal, Carbohydrates:26g, Protein:6g, Fats:8g, Fiber:2g.

6. Wholesome Mushroom Lentil Barley Stew

Yield: 6
Total time: 5 hours and 15 minutes
Ingredients:

- 6-ounce of barley, uncooked
- 6-ounce of lentils, uncooked
- 2 cups of sliced button mushrooms
- 1/2 cup of chopped white onion
- 2 teaspoons of minced garlic
- 1 1/2 teaspoon of salt
- 2 teaspoons of ground black pepper
- 1 teaspoon of dried basil
- 3 bay leaves
- 2 teaspoons of dried savory
- 2 quarts of vegetable broth

Directions:

1. Using a 6-quarts slow cooker, place all the ingredients and stir properly.
2. Cover it with the lid, plug in the slow cooker and let it cook for 5 to 6 hours at the high heat setting or until it is cooked thoroughly.
3. When done, remove the bay leaves and serve.

Nutrition Value:
Calories:179 Cal, Carbohydrates:23g, Protein:6g, Fats:7.4g, Fiber:5.6g.

7. *Tasty Eggplant Stew*

Yield: 6
Total time: 4 hours and 15 minutes
Ingredients:

- 2 medium-sized zucchini, stemmed and sliced
- 1 medium-sized eggplant, peeled and quartered
- 2 medium-sized yellow squash, sliced
- 30 ounce of diced tomatoes
- 4-ounce of sliced mushrooms
- 1 large white onion, peeled and sliced
- 1 tablespoon of minced garlic
- 1 1/2 teaspoon of salt
- 1 tablespoon of dried oregano
- 1 tablespoon of olive oil
- 8 fluid ounce of water

Directions:

1. Using a 6-quarts slow cooker, place all the ingredients and stir properly.
2. Cover it with the lid, plug in the slow cooker and let it cook for 4 hours at the high heat setting or until vegetables get soft.
3. Serve right away.

Nutrition Value:
Calories:62 Cal, Carbohydrates:11g, Protein:2.2g, Fats:2g, Fiber:4g.

8. Satisfying Chipotle Black Bean & Quinoa Stew

Yield: 6
Total time: 5 hours and 15 minutes
Ingredients:

- 1 pound of black beans, uncooked and soaked overnight
- 3/4 cup of quinoa, uncooked and soaked overnight
- 2 dried chipotle peppers
- 28-ounce diced tomatoes
- 1 medium-sized green bell pepper, cored and chopped
- 1 medium-sized red bell pepper, cored and chopped
- 1 medium-sized red onion, peeled and diced
- 1 1/2 teaspoons of minced garlic
- 1 1/2 teaspoon of salt
- 3/4 teaspoon of ground black pepper
- 2 teaspoons of red chili powder
- 1 teaspoon of ground coriander powder
- 1 cinnamon stick, about 3-inch long
- 1/4 cup of chopped cilantro
- 7 cups of water

Directions:

1. Using a 6-quarts slow cooker, place all the ingredients except for salt, cilantro and stir properly.
2. Cover it with the lid, plug in the slow cooker and let it cook for 4 to 5 hours at the high heat setting or until the vegetables get tender.
3. When its 30 minutes to end your cooking, pour in the salt, stir properly and let it cook.
4. When done, garnish it with the cilantro and serve right away.

Nutrition Value:
Calories:120 Cal, Carbohydrates:23g, Protein:6g, Fats:2g, Fiber:5g.

9. Nourishing Lentil Cauliflower Stew

Yield: 6
Total time: 6 hours and 15 minutes
Ingredients:

- 16-ounce of lentils, uncooked and soaked overnight
- 2 cups of chopped kale
- 32 ounce of diced tomatoes
- 1 pound of cauliflower, cut into florets
- 2 leeks, chopped
- 2 large carrots, peeled and chopped
- 3 celery stalks, chopped
- 2 cups of chopped white onion
- 1 teaspoon of minced garlic
- 2 teaspoons of salt
- 1/4 teaspoon of ground black pepper
- 1/2 teaspoon of cayenne
- 1 teaspoon of dried thyme
- 1 teaspoon of ground cumin
- 2 bay leaves
- 1 tablespoon of olive oil
- 2 quarts of vegetable broth

Directions:

1. Place a medium-sized non-stick skillet pan over an average heat, add the oil and let it heat.
2. Add the onion and heat it for 5 minutes or until it gets soft.
3. Then add the garlic and let it cook for 1 minute or until it starts producing fragrance.
4. Transfer this mixture to a 6-quarts slow cooker and add the remaining ingredients.
5. Stir properly and cover it with the lid.
6. Plug in the slow cooker; let it cook for 6 hours at the high heat setting or until the lentils and vegetables get soft.
7. Serve right away.

Nutrition Value:
Calories:222 Cal, Carbohydrates:40g, Protein:12g, Fats:3g, Fiber:13g.

10. Cozy Chickpea Stew

Yield: 6
Total time: 3 hours and 15 minutes
Ingredients:

- 1 cup of chickpeas, uncooked and soaked overnight
- 2 celery stalks, diced
- 1 red pepper, sliced
- 3 medium-sized carrots, peeled and chopped
- 28 ounce of crushed tomatoes
- 2 cups of broccoli florets
- 1 medium-sized white onion, peeled and diced
- 1/2 teaspoon of grated ginger
- 1 teaspoon of minced garlic
- 1 teaspoon of salt
- 1/4 teaspoon of ground black pepper
- 1/8 teaspoon of cayenne pepper
- 1 teaspoon of paprika
- 2 teaspoons of ground cumin
- 1/2 teaspoon of ground cinnamon
- 2 cups of vegetable broth

Directions:

1. Using a 6-quarts slow cooker, place all the ingredients except for salt, cilantro and stir properly.
2. Cover it with the lid, plug in the slow cooker and let it cook for 3 hours at the high heat setting or until the vegetables get soft.
3. When 30 minutes of cooking time is left, pour in the salt, stir properly and let it cook.
4. When done, garnish it with the cilantro and serve right away.

Nutrition Value:
Calories:257 Cal, Carbohydrates:47g, Protein:10g, Fats:4g, Fiber:10g.

TOP SAUCES & CHILI

1. Brilliant Spiced Applesauce

Yield: 24 servings
Total time: 4 hours and 10 minutes
Ingredients:

- 8 apples, peeled and cored
- 1/2 teaspoon pumpkin pie spice
- 6-ounce brown sugar
- 4 fluid ounce water

Directions:

1. Slice apples and place in a 6-quarts slow cooker and add remaining ingredients.
2. Stir until just mix and cover with lid.
3. Plug in the slow cooker and let cook for 3 to 4 hours at high heat setting or until cooked through, stirring every hour.
4. Serve straight away.

Nutrition Value:
Calories:50 Cal, Carbohydrates:13g, Protein:0g, Fats:0g, Fiber:1g.

2. Tangy Tomato Sauce

Yield: 50 servings
Total time: 12 hours and 10 minutes
Ingredients:

- 10 tomatoes, peeled and seeded
- Half of a small white onion, peeled and chopped
- 1 teaspoon of minced garlic
- 1 teaspoon of salt
- 1 teaspoon of ground black pepper
- 1 teaspoon of ground cayenne pepper
- 1 teaspoon of dried oregano
- 1 teaspoon of dried basil
- 1/8 teaspoon of ground cinnamon
- 1/4 cup of olive oil

Directions:

1. Crush the tomatoes and add it to a 6-quarts slow cooker along with the remaining ingredients.
2. Stir properly and cover it with the lid.
3. Plug in the slow cooker and let it cook for 12 hours at the low heat setting or until it is cooked thoroughly, while still stirring occasionally.
4. Let the sauce cool off completely and serve or store in sterilized jars.

Nutrition Value:
Calories:90 Cal, Carbohydrates:13g, Protein:3g, Fats:1g, Fiber:4g.

3. Sweet and Spicy Marinara Sauce

Yield: 40 servings
Total time: 3 hours and 10 minutes
Ingredients:

- 10-ounce frozen spinach, thawed and moisture squeezed out
- 1/3 cup of grated carrot
- 28 ounce of peeled and crushed tomatoes
- 4.5-ounce of sliced mushrooms
- 1 medium-sized white onion, peeled and chopped
- 3 teaspoons of minced garlic
- 2 tablespoons of salt
- 2 tablespoons of dried oregano
- 2 tablespoons of dried basil
- 2 1/2 tablespoons of crushed red pepper
- 2 bay leaves
- 1/4 cup of olive oil
- 8-ounce of tomato paste

Directions:

1. Using a 6-quarts slow cooker, place all the ingredients and stir properly.
2. Cover it with the lid, plug in the slow cooker and let it cook for 3 hours at the low heat setting or until it is cooked thoroughly.
3. Let the sauce cool off completely and serve or store in sterilized jars.

Nutrition Value:
Calories:142 Cal, Carbohydrates:21g, Protein:4g, Fats:5g, Fiber:4g.

4. Rich Spaghetti Sauce

Yield: 60
Total time: 4 hours and 15 minutes
Ingredients:

- 1 medium-sized white onion, peeled and chopped
- 1 1/2 teaspoon of minced garlic
- 3 tablespoons of dried thyme
- 3 tablespoons of dried parsley
- 1/8 teaspoon of crushed red pepper flakes
- 3 tablespoons of dried oregano
- 1 bay leaf
- 145-ounce of tomato sauce
- 18-ounce of tomato paste

Directions:

1. Using a 6-quarts slow cooker, place all the ingredients, and stir properly.
2. Cover it with the lid, plug in the slow cooker and let it cook for 4 hours at the low heat setting or until it is cooked thoroughly.
3. Let the sauce cool off completely and serve or store in sterilized jars.

Nutrition Value:
Calories:92 Cal, Carbohydrates:15g, Protein:2g, Fats:4g, Fiber:3g.

5. Incredible Barbecue Sauce

Yield: 68 servings
Total time: 6 hours and 15 minutes
Ingredients:

- 1/2 cup of chopped white onion
- 1 tablespoon of salt
- 1/4 cup of brown sugar
- 1/2 teaspoon of ground black pepper
- 4 teaspoons of paprika
- 2 tablespoons of molasses
- 1 tablespoon of apple cider vinegar
- 2 tablespoons of Worcestershire sauce
- 1 tablespoon of ground whole-grain mustard paste
- 4 cups of tomato ketchup
- 1/2 cup of water

Directions:

1. Using a 6-quarts slow cooker, place all the ingredients except for the salt, cilantro, and stir properly
2. Cover it with the lid, plug in the slow cooker and let it cook for 6 hours on the low heat setting or until it is cooked thoroughly.
3. When the cooking time is over, with an immersion blender, process the sauce.
4. Then continue cooking for 2 hours. While still stirring occasionally.
5. Let the sauce cool off completely and serve or store in sterilized jars.

Nutrition Value:
Calories:53 Cal, Carbohydrates:12g, Protein:0g, Fats:0.1g, Fiber:0.2g.

6. Flavorful Roasted Red Pepper Sauce

Yield: 6
Total time: 4 hours and 15 minutes
Ingredients:

- 24 ounce of roasted red peppers drained
- 1 large white onion, peeled and sliced
- 1 1/2 teaspoons of minced garlic
- 3/4 teaspoon of salt
- 1/2 teaspoon of ground black pepper
- 1 teaspoon of dried oregano
- 2 cups of tomato passata
- 1/2 cup of cashew cream

Directions:

1. Using a 6-quarts slow cooker, place all the ingredients except for the cream, and stir properly.
2. Cover it with the lid, plug in the slow cooker and let it cook for 4 to 6 hours at the low heat setting or until it is cooked thoroughly.
3. Let the sauce cool off slightly and process it using an immersion blender.
4. Pour in the cream, stir properly and serve the sauce or store in sterilized jars.

Nutrition Value:
Calories:114 Cal, Carbohydrates:6g, Protein:2g, Fats:10g, Fiber:2g.

7. Chunky Pumpkin Spinach Chili

Yield: 6
Total time: 4 hours and 45 minutes
Ingredients:

- 14-ounce of pumpkin
- 1 cup of chopped lady finger
- 1 cup of chopped broccoli
- 28 ounce of diced tomatoes
- 1 medium-sized carrot, peeled and chopped
- 1 small zucchini, stemmed and diced
- 19 ounce of cooked fava beans
- 2 cups of chopped spinach
- 1 small white onion, peeled and diced
- 1 teaspoon of minced garlic
- 1 teaspoon of salt
- 1/2 teaspoon of ground black pepper
- 1 teaspoon red of chili powder
- 2 tablespoons of coconut sugar
- 2 tablespoons of pumpkin pie spice
- 12-ounce of vegetarian ground beef crumbles
- 2 tablespoons of apple cider vinegar
- 8 fluid ounce of vegetable broth

Directions:

1. Using a 6-quarts slow cooker, place all the ingredients except for the beans, spinach, beef crumbles, and stir properly.
2. Cover it with the lid, plug in the slow cooker and let it cook for 3 to 4 hours at the high heat setting or until the vegetables get tender, while still stirring occasionally.
3. Then pour in remaining ingredients, stir properly and continue cooking for 30 minutes.
4. Serve right away.

Nutrition Value:
Calories:177 Cal, Carbohydrates:26g, Protein:2g, Fats:8g, Fiber:5g.

8. Filling Three-Bean Chili

Yield: 8
Total time: 9 hours and 15 minutes
Ingredients:

- 16-ounce of kidney beans, uncooked and soaked overnight
- 16 ounce of cooked whole kernel corn
- 8-ounce of lentils, uncooked and soaked overnight
- 8-ounce of black beans, uncooked and soaked overnight
- 15 ounce of crushed tomatoes
- 3 medium-sized white onions, peeled and chopped
- 1 1/2 teaspoons of minced garlic
- 1 teaspoon of salt
- 1/2 cup of coconut sugar
- 2 tablespoons of red chili powder
- 1 tablespoon of ground cumin
- 1 teaspoon of paprika
- 2 tablespoons of olive oil
- 6-ounce of tomato paste
- 8 cups of water

Directions:

1. Using a 6-quarts slow cooker, place all the ingredients except for the onion, garlic, olive oil, and stir properly.
2. Cover it with the lid, plug in the slow cooker, let it cook for 6 hours at the high heat setting or until the vegetables and beans get soft, while still stirring occasionally.
3. In the meantime, place a medium-sized skillet pan over an average heat, add the oil and let it heat until it gets really hot.
4. Add the onion, garlic and let it cook for 5 minutes or until it getssoft.
5. Add this mixture to the cooked chili and continue cooking for 2 to 3 hours at the high heat setting.
6. Serve right away.

Nutrition Value:
Calories:205 Cal, Carbohydrates:39g, Protein:12g, Fats:2g, Fiber:10g.

9. Comforting Quinoa Chili

Yield: 6
Total time: 4 hours and 15 minutes
Ingredients:

- 16-ounce of black beans, uncooked and rinsed
- 1 cup of quinoa, uncooked and rinsed
- 16-ounce of pinto beans, uncooked and rinsed
- 1 cup of corn kernels, uncooked
- 28 ounce of diced tomatoes
- 1 small white onion, peeled and diced
- 1 1/2 teaspoons of minced garlic
- 1 1/2 tablespoon of taco seasoning
- 1 teaspoon of dried cilantro
- 16-ounce of tomato sauce
- 2 1/2 cups of vegetable broth

Directions:

1. Using a 6-quarts slow cooker, place all the ingredients, and stir properly.
2. Cover with lid, plug in the slow cooker and let it cook for 4 hours at the high heat setting or until it is cooked thoroughly, while stirring occasionally.
3. Garnish it with the vegan Parmesan cheese and serve.

Nutrition Value:
Calories:235 Cal, Carbohydrates:45g, Protein:3g, Fats:8g, Fiber:3g.

10. Sweet Potato Chili

Yield: 4
Total time: 4 hours and 15 minutes
Ingredients:

- 16 black beans, uncooked and rinsed
- 16-ounce of kidney beans, uncooked and rinsed
- 1 medium-sized green bell pepper, cored and chopped
- 8 ounces of sweet potatoes, peeled and chopped
- 28 ounce of diced fire-roasted tomatoes
- 1 medium-sized red onion, peeled and chopped
- 2 teaspoons of minced garlic
- 1 teaspoon of salt
- 1/2 teaspoon of ground black pepper
- 1 tablespoon of red chili powder
- 1 tablespoon of ground cumin
- 1/4 teaspoon of ground cinnamon
- 2 teaspoons of cocoa powder, unsweetened
- 6-ounce of tomato paste
- 8 fluid ounce of water

Directions:

1. Using a 6-quarts slow cooker, place all the ingredients, and stir properly.
2. Cover it with the lid, plug in the slow cooker and let it cook for 4 to 5 hours at the high heat setting or until the vegetables and beans are cooked thoroughly, while stirring occasionally.
3. Garnish it with the vegan Parmesan cheese and serve.

Nutrition Value:
Calories:240 Cal, Carbohydrates:47g, Protein:11g, Fats:2g, Fiber:13g.

ENJOYABLE PIZZAS & GRAINS

1. Fluffy Deep Dish Pizza

Yield: 6
Total time: 2 hours and 15 minutes
Ingredients:

- 12 inch of frozen whole-wheat pizza crust, thawed
- 1 medium-sized red bell pepper, cored and sliced
- 5-ounce of spinach leaves, chopped
- 1 small red onion, peeled and chopped
- 1 1/2 teaspoons of minced garlic
- 1/4 teaspoon of salt
- 1/2 teaspoon of red pepper flakes
- 1/2 teaspoon of dried thyme
- 1/4 cup of chopped basil, fresh
- 14-ounce of pizza sauce
- 1 cup of shredded vegan mozzarella

Directions:

1. Place a medium-sized non-stick skillet pan over an average heat, add the oil and let it heat.
2. Add the onion, garlic and let it cook for 5 minutes or until it gets soft.
3. Then add the red bell pepper and continue cooking for 4 minutes or until it becomes tender-crisp.
4. Add the spinach, salt, red pepper, thyme, basil and stir properly.
5. Cool off for 3 to 5 minutes or until the spinach leaves wilts, and then set it aside until it is called for.
6. Grease a 4-quarts slow cooker with a non-stick cooking spray and insert the pizza crust in it.
7. Press the dough into the bottom and spread 1 inch up along the sides.
8. Spread it with the pizza sauce, cover it with the spinach mixture and then garnish evenly with the cheese.
9. Sprinkle it with the red pepper flakes, basil leaves and cover it with the lid.
10. Plug in the slow cooker and let it cook for 1 1/2 hours to 2 hours at the low heat setting or until the crust turns golden brown and the cheese melts completely.
11. When done, transfer the pizza into the cutting board, let it rest for 10 minutes, then slice to serve.

Nutrition Value:
Calories:250 Cal, Carbohydrates:25g, Protein:5g, Fats:8g, Fiber:1g.

2. Incredible Artichoke and Olives Pizza

Yield: 6
Total time: 1 hours and 50 minutes
Ingredients:

- 12 inch of frozen whole-wheat pizza crust, thawed
- 1 mushroom, sliced
- 1/2 cup of sliced char-grilled artichokes
- 1 small green bell pepper, cored and sliced
- 2 medium-sized tomatoes, sliced
- 2 tablespoons of sliced black olives
- 1/2 teaspoon of garlic powder
- 1 teaspoon of salt, divided
- 1/2 teaspoon of dried oregano
- 2 tablespoons of nutritional yeast
- 2-ounce cashews
- 2 teaspoons of lemon juice
- 3 tablespoon of olive oil, divided
- 8-ounce of tomato paste
- 4 fluid ounce of water

Directions:

1. Place the cashews in a food processor; add the garlic powder, 1/2 teaspoon of salt, yeast, 2 tablespoons of oil, lemon juice, and water.
2. Mash it until it gets smooth and creamy, but add some water if need be.
3. Grease a 4 to 6 quarts slow cooker with a non-stick cooking spray and insert the pizza crust into it.
4. Press the dough in bottom and spread the tomato paste on top of it.
5. Sprinkle it with garlic powder, oregano and top it with the prepared cashew mixture.
6. Spray it with the mushrooms, bell peppers, tomato, artichoke slices, olives and then with the remaining olive oil.
7. Sprinkle it with the oregano, the remaining salt and cover it with the lid.
8. Plug in the slow cooker and let it cook for 1 to 1 1/2 hours at the low heat setting or until the crust turns golden brown.
9. When done, transfer the pizza to the cutting board, let it rest for 10 minutes and slice to serve.

Nutrition Value:
Calories:212 Cal, Carbohydrates:39g, Protein:16g, Fats:5g, Fiber:5g.

3. _Mushroom and Peppers Pizza_

Yield: 6
Total time: 2 hours
Ingredients:

- 12 inch of frozen whole-wheat pizza crust, thawed
- 1/2 cup of chopped red bell pepper
- 1/2 cup of chopped green bell pepper
- 1/2 cup of chopped orange bell pepper
- 3/4 cup of chopped button mushrooms
- 1 small red onion, peeled and chopped
- 1 teaspoon of garlic powder, divided
- 1 teaspoon of salt, divided
- 1/2 teaspoon of coconut sugar
- 1/2 teaspoon of red pepper flakes
- 1 teaspoon of dried basil, divided
- 1 1/2 teaspoon of dried oregano, divided
- 1 tablespoon of olive oil
- 6-ounce of tomato paste
- 1/2 cup of vegan Parmesan cheese

Directions:

1. Place a large non-stick skillet pan over an average heat, add the oil and let it heat.
2. Add the onion, bell peppers and cook for 10 minutes or until it gets soft and lightly charred. Then add the mushroom, cook it for 3 minutes and set the pan aside until it is needed.
3. Pour the tomato sauce, sugar, 1/2 teaspoon of the garlic powder, salt, basil, oregano, into a bowl and stir properly.
4. Grease a 4 to 6 quarts slow cooker with a non-stick cooking spray and insert the pizza crust into it.
5. Press the dough in bottom and spread the already prepared tomato sauce on top of it. Sprinkle it with the Parmesan cheese and top it with the cooked vegetable mixture.
6. Cover it with the lid, plug in the slow cooker and let it cook for 1 to 1 1/2 hours at the low heat setting or until the crust turns golden brown.
7. When done, transfer the pizza to a cutting board, sprinkle it with the remaining oregano, basil, then let it rest for 10 minutes and then slice to serve.

Nutrition Value:
Calories:188 Cal, Carbohydrates:27g, Protein:5g, Fats:5g, Fiber:3g.

4. Tangy Barbecue Tofu Pizza

Yield: 6
Total time: 2 hours
Ingredients:

- 12 inch of frozen whole-wheat pizza crust, thawed
- 1 cup of tofu pieces
- 1 small red onion, peeled and sliced
- 1/4 cup of chopped cilantro
- 1 1/2 teaspoons of salt
- 3/4 teaspoon of ground black pepper
- 1 tablespoon of olive oil
- 1 cup of barbecue sauce
- 2 cups of vegan mozzarella

Directions:

1. Place a large non-stick skillet pan over an average heat, add 1 tablespoon of oil and let it heat.
2. Add the tofu pieces in a single layer sprinkle it with 1 teaspoon of salt, black pepper and cook for 5 to 7 minutes or until it gets crispy with a golden brown on all sides.
3. Transfer the tofu pieces into a bowl, add 1/2 cup of the barbecue sauce and toss it properly to coat.
4. Grease a 4 to 6 quarts slow cooker with a non-stick cooking spray and insert the pizza crust in it.
5. Press the dough into the bottom and spread the remaining 1/2 cup of the barbecue sauce.
6. Evenly garnish it with tofu pieces and onion slices.
7. Sprinkle it with the mozzarella cheese and cover it with the lid.
8. Plug in the slow cooker and let it cook for 1 to 1 1/2 hours at the low heat setting or until the crust turns golden brown.
9. When done, transfer the pizza into the cutting board, let it rest for 10 minutes and slice to serve.

Nutrition Value:
Calories:135 Cal, Carbohydrates:15g, Protein:6g, Fats:5g, Fiber:1g.

5. Tasty Tomato Garlic Mozzarella Pizza

Yield: 6   **Total time: 2 hours and 30 minutes**

Ingredients:

- 12 inch of frozen whole-wheat pizza crust, thawed
- 3/4 teaspoon of tapioca flour
- 2 teaspoons of minced garlic
- 2 teaspoons of agar powder
- 1 teaspoon of cornstarch
- 1 teaspoon of salt, divided
- 1/2 teaspoon of red pepper flakes

- 1/2 teaspoon of dried basil
- 1/2 teaspoon of dried parsley
- 2 tablespoons of olive oil
- 1/4 teaspoon of lemon juice
- 3/4 teaspoon of apple cider vinegar
- 8 fluid ounce of coconut milk, unsweetened

Directions:

1. Start by preparing the mozzarella.
2. Place a small saucepan over a medium-low heat, pour in the milk and let it steam until it gets warm thoroughly.
3. With a whisker, pour in the agar powder and stir properly until it dissolves completely.
4. Switch the temperature to a low and pour in the salt, lemon juice, vinegar, and whisk them properly.
5. Mix the tapioca flour and cornstarch with 2 tablespoons of water before adding it to the milk mixture.
6. Whisk properly and transfer this mixture to a greased bowl.
7. Place the bowl in a refrigerator for 1 hour or until it is set.
8. Then grease a- 4 to 6 quarts of the slow cooker with a non-stick cooking spray and insert pizza crust into it.
9. Press the dough into the bottom and brush the top with olive oil.
10. Spread the garlic and then cover it with the tomato slices.
11. Sprinkle it with salt, red pepper flakes, basil, and the oregano.
12. Cut the mozzarella cheese into coins and place them across the top of the pizza.
13. Cover it with the lid, plug in the slow cooker, let it cook for 1 to 1 1/2 hours at the low heat setting or until the crust turns golden brown and the cheese melts completely. When done, transfer the pizza to the cutting board, then let it rest for 5 minutes, and slice to serve.

Nutrition Value:
Calories:113 Cal, Carbohydrates:10g, Protein:7g, Fats:5g, Fiber:1g.

6. Delicious Chipotle Red Lentil Pizza

Yield: 4
Total time: 1 hours and 45 minutes
Ingredients:

- 12 inch of frozen whole-wheat pizza crust, thawed
- 1/4 cup of red lentils, uncooked and rinsed
- 1/4 cup of chopped carrot
- 1 cups of chopped tomato
- 1 medium-sized tomatoes, sliced
- 2 green onions, sliced
- 1 chipotle chili pepper in adobo sauce. Chopped
- 1/2 cup of sliced olives
- 1/4 cup of chopped red onion
- 1/2 teaspoon of minced garlic
- 1/2 teaspoon of salt
- 1/4 teaspoon of ground black pepper
- 1/2 teaspoon of cayenne pepper
- 1/2 teaspoon of dried oregano
- 1 teaspoon of dried basil, divided
- 1 tablespoon of tomato paste
- 1 teaspoon of olive oil
- 1/2 teaspoon of apple cider vinegar
- 1 cup of water
- 1 cup crumbled almond ricotta cheese

Directions:

1. Place a medium-sized non-stick skillet pan over an average heat, add the oil and let it heat.
2. Add the onion, garlic and using the sauté button, heat it for 5 minutes or until the onions get soft.
3. Add the carrots, tomatoes, chipotle chile, oregano, 1/2 teaspoon of basil and stir properly.
4. Let it cook for 5 minutes before adding the lentils, salt, black pepper, cayenne pepper, vinegar, and water.

5. Stir properly, cook for 15 to 20 minutes or until the lentils get tender, thereafter, cover the pan partially with a lid.
14. In the meantime, grease a 4 to 6 quarts slow cooker with a non-stick cooking spray and insert pizza crust into it.
6. Press the dough into the bottom and spread the lentil mixture.
7. Spray it with the tomato slices, green onions, and olives.
8. Spread the cheese over the top and sprinkle it with the remaining 1/2 teaspoon of basil.
9. Cover it with the lid, plug in the slow cooker and let it cook for 1 hour or until the crust turns golden brown and allow the cheese to melt completely.
10. When done, transfer the pizza to the cutting board, then let it rest for 5 minutes, before slicing to serve.

Nutrition Value:
Calories:369 Cal, Carbohydrates:56g, Protein:5g, Fats:15g, Fiber:5g.

7. Nourishing Whole-Grain Porridge

Yield: 4
Total time: 2 hours and 10 minutes
Ingredients:

- 3/4 cup of steel-cut oats, rinsed and soaked overnight
- 3/4 cup of whole barley, rinsed and soaked overnight
- 1/2 cup of cornmeal
- 1 teaspoon of salt
- 3 tablespoons of brown sugar
- 1 cinnamon stick, about 3 inches long
- 1 teaspoon of vanilla extract, unsweetened
- 4 1/2 cups of water

Directions:

1. Using a 6-quarts slow cooker, place all the ingredients and stir properly.
2. Cover it with the lid, plug in the slow cooker and let it cook for 2 hours or until grains get soft, while stirring halfway through.
3. Serve the porridge with fruits.

Nutrition Value:
Calories:129 Cal, Carbohydrates:22g, Protein:5g, Fats:2g, Fiber:4g.

8. Pungent Mushroom Barley Risotto

Yield: 4
Total time: 3 hours and 30 minutes
Ingredients:

- 1 1/2 cups of hulled barley, rinsed and soaked overnight
- 8 ounces of carrots, peeled and chopped
- 1 pound of mushrooms, sliced
- 1 large white onion, peeled and chopped
- 3/4 teaspoon of salt
- 1/2 teaspoon of ground black pepper
- 4 sprigs thyme
- 1/4 cup of chopped parsley
- 2/3 cup of grated vegetarian Parmesan cheese
- 1 tablespoon of apple cider vinegar
- 2 tablespoons of olive oil
- 1 1/2 cups of vegetable broth

Directions:

1. Place a large non-stick skillet pan over a medium-high heat, add the oil and let it heat until it gets hot.
2. Add the onion along with 1/4 teaspoon of each the salt and black pepper.
3. Cook it for 5 minutes or until it turns golden brown.
4. Then add the mushrooms and continue cooking for 2 minutes.
5. Add the barley, thyme and cook for another 2 minutes.
6. Transfer this mixture to a 6-quarts slow cooker and add the carrots, 1/4 teaspoon of salt, and the vegetable broth.
7. Stir properly and cover it with the lid.
8. Plug in the slow cooker, let it cook for 3 hours at the high heat setting or until the grains absorb all the cooking liquid and the vegetables get soft.
9. Remove the thyme sprigs, pour in the remaining ingredients except for parsley and stir properly.
10. Pour in the warm water and stir properly until the risotto reaches your desired state.
11. Add the seasoning, then garnish it with parsley and serve.

Nutrition Value:
Calories:321 Cal, Carbohydrates:48g, Protein:12g, Fats:10g, Fiber:11g.

9. Healthful Lentil and Rice Stew

Yield: 6
Total time: 4 hours and 15 minutes
Ingredients:

- 1/2 cup of brown rice, rinsed
- 1 cup of brown lentils, rinsed
- 1 cup of chopped white onion
- 3/4 teaspoon of salt
- 1 teaspoon of ground turmeric
- 1 tablespoon of ground cumin
- 1/2 teaspoon of ground cinnamon
- 1 1/2 tablespoons of olive oil
- 1 1/2 quarts of water

Directions:

1. Place a medium-sized non-stick skillet pan over a medium heat, add the oil and let it heat.
2. Add the onion and using the sauté button, heat it for 5 minutes or until it turns golden brown.
3. Transfer this mixture to a 6-quarts slow cooker, pour in the remaining ingredients and cover it with the lid.
4. Plug in the slow cooker and let it cook for 3 to 4 hours at the high heat setting or until the grains get soft.
5. Garnish it with the cilantro and serve it with lemon wedges.

Nutrition Value:
Calories:369 Cal, Carbohydrates:56g, Protein:5g, Fats:15g, Fiber:5g.

10. Remarkable Three-Grain Medley

Yield: 6
Total time: 3 hours and 15 minutes
Ingredients:

- 1/2 cup of uncooked hulled barley, rinsed and soaked overnight
- 1/2 cup of uncooked wild rice, rinse and soaked overnight
- 2/3 cup of uncooked wheat berries, rinsed and soaked overnight
- 1/2 cup of sliced green onions
- 1 teaspoon of minced garlic
- 1/4 cup of chopped parsley
- 2 teaspoons of shredded lemon peel
- 1/4 cup of olive oil
- 28-ounce of vegetable broth
- 2 ounces of diced cherry pepper

Directions:

1. Place all the ingredients in a 6-quarts slow cooker and stir properly.
2. Cover it with the lid, plug in the slow cooker and let it cook for 2 to 3 hours at the high heat setting or until the grains absorbs all the liquid, as a result becoming soft.
3. Serve right away.

Nutrition Value:
Calories:200 Cal, Carbohydrates:38g, Protein:5g, Fats:3g, Fiber:3g.

11. Hearty Millet Stew

Yield: 4
Total time: 4 hours and 30 minutes
Ingredients:

- 1 cup of millet, uncooked
- 2 medium-sized potatoes, peeled and chopped
- 2 medium-sized carrots, peeled and chopped
- 1 cup of celery, chopped
- 1/2 pound of mushrooms, chopped
- 2 medium-sized white onions, peeled and sliced
- 1 teaspoon of minced garlic
- 1 teaspoon of salt
- 1/2 teaspoon of ground black pepper
- 1/2 teaspoon of dried basil
- 1/2 teaspoon of dried thyme
- 2 bay leaves
- 4 cups of water

Directions:

1. Place a medium-sized non-stick skillet pan over an average heat, add the millet and let it cook for 5 minutes or until it gets toasted, while stirring frequently.
2. Transfer the toasted millets to a 6-quarts slow cooker, and reserve the pan.
3. Add the potatoes, carrots, celery, mushrooms and onion to the pan and let it cook for 5 to 7 minutes or until it is properly toasted.
4. Transfer the veggies to the slow cooker, pour in the remaining ingredients, stir and cover it with the lid.
5. Then plug in the slow cooker and let it cook for 4 hours at the high heat setting or until the vegetables and grains are cooked thoroughly.
6. Serve right away.

Nutrition Value:
Calories:268 Cal, Carbohydrates:44g, Protein:8g, Fats:6g, Fiber:8g.

GRACEFUL VEGETABLES

1. Scrumptious Baked Potatoes

Yield: 8
Total time: 8 hours and 10 minutes
Ingredients:

- 8 potatoes
- Salt to taste for serving
- Ground black pepper to taste for serving

Directions:

1. Rinse potatoes until clean, wipe dry and then prick with a fork.
2. Wrap each potato in an aluminum foil and place in a 6 to 8 quarts slow cooker.
3. Cover with lid, and then plug in the slow cooker and let cook on low heat setting for 8 hours or until tender.
4. When the cooking time is over, unwrap potatoes and prick with a fork to check if potatoes are tender or not.
5. Sprinkle potatoes with salt, black pepper, and your favorite seasoning and serve.

Nutrition Value:
Calories:93 Cal, Carbohydrates:3g, Protein:3g, Fats:1g, Fiber:2g.

2. Fantastic Butternut Squash & Vegetables

Yield: 6
Total time: 4 hours and 15 minutes
Ingredients:

- 1 1/2 cups of corn kernels
- 2 pounds of butternut squash
- 1 medium-sized green bell pepper
- 14 1/2 ounce of diced tomatoes
- 1/2 cup of chopped white onion
- 1/2 teaspoon of minced garlic
- 1/2 teaspoon of salt
- 1/4 teaspoon of ground black pepper
- 1 tablespoon and 2 teaspoons of tomato paste
- 1/2 cup of vegetable broth

Directions:

1- Peel, centralize the butternut squash and dice, and place it into a 6-quarts slow cooker.
2- Create a hole on the green bell pepper, then cut it into 1/2 inch pieces and add it to the slow cooker.
3- Add the remaining ingredients into the slow cooker except for tomato paste, stir properly and cover it with the lid.
4- Then plug in the slow cooker and let it cook on the low heat setting for 6 hours or until the vegetables get soft.
5- When 6 hours of the cooking time is done, remove 1/2 cup of the cooking liquid from the slow cooker.
6- Then pour the tomatoes mixture into this cooking liquid, stir properly and place it in the slow cooker.
7- Stir properly and continue cooking for 30 minutes or until the mixture becomes slightly thick.
8- Serve right away.

Nutrition Value:
Calories:134 Cal, Carbohydrates:23g, Protein:6g, Fats:2g, Fiber:4g.

3. *Fabulous Glazed Carrots*

Yield: 5
Total time: 2 hours and 20 minutes
Ingredients:

- 1 pound of carrots
- 2 teaspoons of chopped cilantro
- 1/4 teaspoon of salt
- 1/4 cup of brown sugar
- 1/4 teaspoon of ground cinnamon
- 1/8 teaspoon of ground nutmeg
- 1 tablespoon of cornstarch
- 1 tablespoon of olive oil
- 2 tablespoons of water
- 1 large orange, juiced and zested

Directions:

1- Peel the carrots, rinse, cut it into 1/4 inch thick rounds and place it in a 6 quarts slow cooker.
2- Add the salt, sugar, cinnamon, nutmeg, olive oil, orange zest, juice, and stir properly.
3- Cover it with the lid, then plug in the slow cooker and let it cook on the high heat setting for 2 hours or until the carrots become soft.
4- Stir properly the cornstarch and water until it blends well. Thereafter, add this mixture to the slow cooker.
5- Continue cooking for 10 minutes or until the sauce in the slow cooker gets slightly thick.
6- Sprinkle the cilantro over carrots and serve.

Nutrition Value:
Calories:160 Cal, Carbohydrates:40g, Protein:1g, Fats:0.3g, Fiber:2.3g.

4. Flavorful Sweet Potatoes with Apples

Yield: 6
Total time: 5 hours
Ingredients:

- 3 medium-sized apples, peeled and cored
- 6 medium-sized sweet potatoes, peeled and cored
- 1/4 cup of pecans
- 1/4 teaspoon of ground cinnamon
- 1/4 teaspoon of ground nutmeg
- 2 tablespoons of vegan butter, melted
- 1/4 cup of maple syrup

Directions:

1- Cut the sweet potatoes and the apples into 1/2 inch slices.
2- Grease a 6-quarts slow cooker with a non-stick cooking spray and arrange the sweet potato slices in the bottom of the cooker.
3- Top it with the apple slices; sprinkle it with the cinnamon and nutmeg, before garnishing it with butter.
4- Cover it with the lid, plug in the slow cooker and let it cook on the low heat setting for 4 hours or until the sweet potatoes get soft.
5- When done, sprinkle it with pecan and continue cooking for another 30 minutes.
6- Serve right away.

Nutrition Value:
Calories:120 Cal, Carbohydrates:24g, Protein:1g, Fats:3g, Fiber:2g.

5. Fuss-Free Cabbage and Tomatoes Stew

Yield: 6
Total time: 3 hours and 10 minutes
Ingredients:

- 1 medium-sized cabbage head, chopped
- 1 medium-sized white onion, peeled and sliced
- 28-ounce of stewed tomatoes
- 3/4 teaspoon of salt
- 1/4 teaspoon of ground black pepper
- 10-ounce of tomato soup

Directions:

1- Using a 6 quarts slow cooker, place all the ingredients and stir properly.
2- Cover it with the lid, plug in the slow cooker and let it cook at the high heat setting for 3 hours or until the vegetables gets soft.
3- Serve right away.

Nutrition Value:
Calories:103 Cal, Carbohydrates:17g, Protein:4g, Fats:2g, Fiber:4g.

6. Wonderful Glazed Root Vegetables

Yield: 6
Total time: 4 hours and 20 minutes
Ingredients:

- 6 medium-sized carrots
- 4 medium-sized parsnips
- 1 pound of sweet potatoes
- 2 medium-sized red onions
- 1 teaspoon of salt
- 1/2 teaspoon of ground black pepper
- 5 teaspoons of chopped thyme
- 3 tablespoons of honey
- 1 tablespoon of apple cider vinegar
- 1 tablespoon of olive oil

Directions:

1. Peel the carrots, parsnip, sweet potatoes, onions, and cut it into 1-inch pieces.
2. Grease a 6 quarts slow cooker with a non-stick cooking spray, place the carrots, parsnip, onion in the bottom and then top it with the sweet potatoes.
3. Using a bowl whisk the salt, black pepper, 2 teaspoons of thyme, honey and oil properly.
4. Pour this mixture over on the vegetables and toss it to coat.
5. Cover it with the lid, then plug in the slow cooker and let it cook at the low heat setting for 4 hours or until the vegetables get tender.
6. When cooked, pour in the vinegar, stir, sprinkle it with the remaining thyme and serve.

Nutrition Value:
Calories:137 Cal, Carbohydrates:26g, Protein:2g, Fats:4g, Fiber:3g.

7. Super Aubergines

Yield: 6
Total time: 8 hours and 15 minutes
Ingredients:

- 1 pound of eggplant
- 10-ounce of tomatoes, quartered
- 2-ounce of sun-dried tomatoes
- 1 small fennel bulb, sliced
- 1 medium-sized red onion, peeled and sliced
- 1/2 cup of chopped parsley
- 1/4 cup of chopped basil
- 1/4 cup of chopped chives
- 2 teaspoons of capers
- 1 teaspoon of minced garlic
- 1 1/2 teaspoon of salt
- 1 teaspoon of ground black pepper
- 1 teaspoon of coriander seeds
- 1 lemon, juiced
- 6 tablespoons of olive oil, divided

Directions:

1. Using a 6 quarts slow cooker, add 2 tablespoons of olive oil, top it with onions and garlic.
2. Remove the stem of the eggplant, cut it into 1/2-inch thick slices and brush 2 tablespoons oil on both sides of the eggplant slices.
3. Garnish the onion with the eggplant slices and cover it with tomato pieces, sun-dried tomatoes, and fennel slices.
4. Sprinkle it with salt, black pepper, and coriander seeds.
5. Cover it with the lid, then plug in the slow cooker and let it cook at the low heat setting for 6 to 8 hours or until vegetables gets tender.
6. While doing that, place the parsley, basil and chives in a food processor.
7. Add the remaining 2 tablespoons of olive oil along with the lemon juice, caper, and pulse it until it gets smooth.
8. When the vegetables are cooked, transfer it to a serving platter and drizzle it with the prepared herbs mixture.
9. Serve right away with crusty bread.

Nutrition Value:
Calories:62 Cal, Carbohydrates:12g, Protein:2g, Fats:2g, Fiber:4g.

8. Sweet and Spicy Red Thai Vegetable Curry

Yield: 6
Total time: 4 hours and 45 minutes
Ingredients:

- 1/2 head cauliflower, chopped into florets
- 2 medium-sized sweet potatoes, peeled and cubed
- 1 cup of cooked green peas
- 8 ounce of chopped white mushrooms
- 1/4 cup of chopped cilantro, chopped
- 1 small white onion, sliced
- 1/2 teaspoon of salt
- 1 tablespoon of brown sugar
- 1/2 cup of toasted cashews
- 3 tablespoon of red curry paste
- 3 tablespoons of soy sauce
- 2 teaspoons of Sriracha sauce
- 14-ounce of coconut milk

Directions:

1. Grease a 6-quarts slow cooker with a non-stick cooking spray and add the cauliflower florets, sweet potatoes, and onion.
2. Using a bowl, stir properly the salt, sugar, red curry paste, soy sauce, Sriracha sauce and thr coconut milk.
3. Pour this mixture on top of the vegetables in the slow cooker and toss it to coat properly.
4. Cover it with the lid, then plug in the slow cooker and let it cook at the low heat setting for 4 hours or until the vegetables get soft.
5. Then add the mushrooms, peas, to the slow cooker and continue cooking for 30 minutes.
6. Garnish it with cilantro and serve.

Nutrition Value:
Calories:141 Cal, Carbohydrates:13g, Protein:0g, Fats:9g, Fiber:3g.

9. Vibrant Minestrone

Yield: 6
Total time: 6 hours and 25 minutes
Ingredients:

- 30 ounce of cooked cannellini beans
- 8 ounces of uncooked small pasta
- 12 thins of asparagus spears
- 3 carrots, peeled and sliced
- 6 ounce of chopped spinach
- 28 ounce of diced tomatoes
- 1 cup of cooked peas
- 1 medium-sized white onion, peeled and diced
- 1 1/2 teaspoon of minced garlic
- 1 teaspoon of salt
- 1/2 teaspoon of ground black pepper
- 3 cups of vegetable stock
- 3 cups of water
- 1/3 cup of grated parmesan cheese

Directions:

1. Grease a 6-quarts slow cooker with a non-stick cooking spray, add the beans, carrots, tomatoes, onion, garlic, vegetable stock and water.
2. Stir properly and cover it with the lid.
3. Then plug in the slow cooker and let it cook at the low heat setting for 4 hours or until the vegetables get soft.
4. While doing that cut the asparagus into three and when the vegetables are cooked add the asparagus to the slow cooker along with the peas, salt, black pepper, spinach, and pasta.
5. Continue cooking for 15 minutes.
6. Garnish it with cheese and serve.

Nutrition Value:
Calories:110 Cal, Carbohydrates:18g, Protein:5g, Fats:2g, Fiber:4g.

10. Awesome Spinach Artichoke Soup

Yield: 6
Total time: 4 hours and 45 minutes
Ingredients:

- 15 ounce of cooked white beans
- 2 cups of frozen artichoke hearts, thawed
- 2 cups of spinach leaves
- 1 small red onion, peeled and chopped
- 1 teaspoon of minced garlic
- 1 teaspoon of salt
- 1/2 teaspoon of ground black pepper
- 2 teaspoons of dried basil
- 1 teaspoon of dried oregano
- 1/2 teaspoon of whole-grain mustard paste
- 2 1/2 tablespoons of nutritional yeast
- 1 1/2 teaspoons of white miso
- 4 tablespoons of lemon juice
- 16 fluid ounce of almond milk, unsweetened
- 3 cups of vegetable broth
- 1 cups of water

Directions:

1. Grease a 6-quarts slow cooker with a non-stick cooking spray, add the artichokes, spinach, onion, garlic, salt, black pepper, basil, and the oregano.
2. Pour in the vegetable broth and water, stir properly and cover it with the lid.
3. Then plug in the slow cooker and let it cook at the high heat setting for 4 hours or until the vegetables get soft.
4. While waiting for that, place the white beans in a food processor, add the yeast, miso, mustard, lemon juice and almond milk.
5. Mash until it gets smooth, and set it aside.
6. When the vegetables are cooked thoroughly, add the prepared bean mixture and continue cooking for 30 minutes at the high heat setting or until the soup gets slightly thick.
7. Garnish it with cheese and serve.

Nutrition Value:
Calories:200 Cal, Carbohydrates:13g, Protein:4g, Fats:12g, Fiber:2g.

MOUTH-WATERING DRINKS

1. Energizing Ginger Detox Tonic

Yield: 2
Total time: 15 minutes
Ingredients:

- 1/2 teaspoon of grated ginger, fresh
- 1 small lemon slice
- 1/8 teaspoon of cayenne pepper
- 1/8 teaspoon of ground turmeric
- 1/8 teaspoon of ground cinnamon
- 1 teaspoon of maple syrup
- 1 teaspoon of apple cider vinegar
- 2 cups of boiling water

Directions:

1. Pour the boiling water into a small saucepan, add and stir the ginger, then let it rest for 8 to 10 minutes, before covering the pan.
2. Pass the mixture through a strainer and into the liquid, add the cayenne pepper, turmeric, cinnamon and stir properly.
3. Add the maple syrup, vinegar, and lemon slice.
4. Add and stir an infused lemon and serve immediately.

Nutrition Value:
Calories:80 Cal, Carbohydrates:0g, Protein:0g, Fats:0g, Fiber:0g.

2. Warm Spiced Lemon Drink

Yield: 12
Total time: 2 hours and 10 minutes
Ingredients:

- 1 cinnamon stick, about 3 inches long
- 1/2 teaspoon of whole cloves
- 2 cups of coconut sugar
- 4 fluid of ounce pineapple juice
- 1/2 cup and 2 tablespoons of lemon juice
- 12 fluid ounce of orange juice
- 2 1/2 quarts of water

Directions:

1. Pour water into a 6-quarts slow cooker and stir the sugar and lemon juice properly.
2. Wrap the cinnamon, the whole cloves in cheesecloth and tie its corners with string.
3. Immerse this cheesecloth bag in the liquid present in the slow cooker and cover it with the lid.
4. Then plug in the slow cooker and let it cook on high heat setting for 2 hours or until it is heated thoroughly.
5. When done, discard the cheesecloth bag and serve the drink hot or cold.

Nutrition Value:
Calories:15 Cal, Carbohydrates:3.2g, Protein:0.1g, Fats:0g, Fiber:0g.

3. Soothing Ginger Tea Drink

Yield: 8
Total time: 2 hours and 15 minutes
Ingredients:

- 1 tablespoon of minced gingerroot
- 2 tablespoons of honey
- 15 green tea bags
- 32 fluid ounce of white grape juice
- 2 quarts of boiling water

Directions:

1. Pour water into a 4-quarts slow cooker, immerse tea bags, cover the cooker and let stand for 10 minutes.
2. After 10 minutes, remove and discard tea bags and stir in remaining ingredients.
3. Return cover to slow cooker, then plug in and let cook at high heat setting for 2 hours or until heated through.
4. When done, strain the liquid and serve hot or cold.

Nutrition Value:
Calories:45 Cal, Carbohydrates:12g, Protein:0g, Fats:0g, Fiber:0g.

4. Nice Spiced Cherry Cider

Yield: 16
Total time: 4 hours and 5 minutes
Ingredients:

- 2 cinnamon sticks, each about 3 inches long
- 6-ounce of cherry gelatin
- 4 quarts of apple cider

Directions:

1. Using a 6-quarts slow cooker, pour the apple cider and add the cinnamon stick.
2. Stir, then cover the slow cooker with its lid. Plug in the cooker and let it cook for 3 hours at the high heat setting or until it is heated thoroughly.
3. Then add and stir the gelatin properly, then continue cooking for another hour.
4. When done, remove the cinnamon sticks and serve the drink hot or cold.

Nutrition Value: ,
Calories:100 Cal, Carbohydrates:0g, Protein:0g, Fats:0g, Fiber:0g.

5. *Fragrant Spiced Coffee*

Yield: 8
Total time: 2 hours and 10 minutes
Ingredients:

- 4 cinnamon sticks, each about 3 inches long
- 1 1/2 teaspoons of whole cloves
- 1/3 cup of honey
- 2-ounce of chocolate syrup
- 1/2 teaspoon of anise extract
- 8 cups of brewed coffee

Directions:

1. Pour the coffee in a 4-quarts slow cooker and pour in the remaining ingredients except for cinnamon and stir properly.
2. Wrap the whole cloves in cheesecloth and tie its corners with strings.
3. Immerse this cheesecloth bag in the liquid present in the slow cooker and cover it with the lid.
4. Then plug in the slow cooker and let it cook on the low heat setting for 3 hours or until heated thoroughly.
5. When done, discard the cheesecloth bag and serve.

Nutrition Value:
Calories:150 Cal, Carbohydrates:35g, Protein:3g, Fats:0g, Fiber:0g.

6. Tangy Spiced Cranberry Drink

Yield: 14
Total time: 2 hours and 10 minutes
Ingredients:

- 1 1/2 cups of coconut sugar
- 12 whole cloves
- 2 fluid ounce of lemon juice
- 6 fluid ounce of orange juice
- 32 fluid ounce of cranberry juice
- 8 cups of hot water
- 1/2 cup of Red Hot candies

Directions:

1. Pour the water into a 6-quarts slow cooker along with the cranberry juice, orange juice, and the lemon juice.
2. Stir the sugar properly.
3. Wrap the whole cloves in a cheese cloth, tie its corners with strings, and immerse it in the liquid present inside the slow cooker.
4. Add the red hot candies to the slow cooker and cover it with the lid.
6. Then plug in the slow cooker and let it cook on the low heat setting for 3 hours or until it is heated thoroughly.
5. When done, discard the cheesecloth bag and serve.

Nutrition Value:
Calories:89 Cal, Carbohydrates:27g, Protein:0g, Fats:0g, Fiber:1g.

7. Warm Pomegranate Punch

Yield: 10
Total time: 2 hours and 15 minutes
Ingredients:

- 3 cinnamon sticks, each about 3 inches long
- 12 whole cloves
- 1/2 cup of coconut sugar
- 1/3 cup of lemon juice
- 32 fluid ounce of pomegranate juice
- 32 fluid ounce of apple juice, unsweetened
- 16 fluid ounce of brewed tea

Directions:

1. Using a 4-quart slow cooker, pour the lemon juice, pomegranate, juice apple juice, tea, and then sugar.
2. Wrap the whole cloves and cinnamon stick in a cheese cloth, tie its corners with a string, and immerse it in the liquid present in the slow cooker.
3. Then cover it with the lid, plug in the slow cooker and let it cook at the low heat setting for 3 hours or until it is heated thoroughly.
4. When done, discard the cheesecloth bag and serve it hot or cold.

Nutrition Value:
Calories:253 Cal, Carbohydrates:58g, Protein:7g, Fats:2g, Fiber:3g.

8. Rich Truffle Hot Chocolate

Yield: 4
Total time: 1 hours and 10 minutes
Ingredients:

- 1/3 cup of cocoa powder, unsweetened
- 1/3 cup of coconut sugar
- 1/8 teaspoon of salt
- 1/8 teaspoon of ground cinnamon
- 1 teaspoon of vanilla extract, unsweetened
- 32 fluid ounce of coconut milk

Directions:

1. Using a 2 quarts slow cooker, add all the ingredients and stir properly.
2. Cover it with the lid, then plug in the slow cooker and cook it for 2 hours on the high heat setting or until it is heated thoroughly.
3. When done, serve right away.

Nutrition Value:
Calories:67 Cal, Carbohydrates:13g, Protein:2g, Fats:2g, Fiber:2.3g.

9. Ultimate Mulled Wine

Yield: 6
Total time: 35 minutes
Ingredients:

- 1 cup of cranberries, fresh
- 2 oranges, juiced
- 1 tablespoon of whole cloves
- 2 cinnamon sticks, each about 3 inches long
- 1 tablespoon of star anise
- 1/3 cup of honey
- 8 fluid ounce of apple cider
- 8 fluid ounce of cranberry juice
- 24 fluid ounce of red wine

Directions:

1. Using a 4 quarts slow cooker, add all the ingredients and stir properly.
2. Cover it with the lid, then plug in the slow cooker and cook it for 30 minutes on thee high heat setting or until it gets warm thoroughly.
3. When done, strain the wine and serve right away.

Nutrition Value:
Calories:202 Cal, Carbohydrates:25g, Protein:0g, Fats:0g, Fiber:0g.

10. Pleasant Lemonade

Yield: 10 servings
Total time: 3 hours and 15 minutes
Ingredients:

- Cinnamon sticks for serving
- 2 cups of coconut sugar
- 1/4 cup of honey
- 3 cups of lemon juice. fresh
- 32 fluid ounce of water

Directions:

1. Using a 4-quarts slow cooker, place all the ingredients except for the cinnamon sticks and stir properly.
2. Cover it with the lid, then plug in the slow cooker and cook it for 3 hours on the low heat setting or until it is heated thoroughly.
3. When done, stir properly and serve with the cinnamon sticks.

Nutrition Value:
Calories:146 Cal, Carbohydrates:34g, Protein:0g, Fats:0g, Fiber:0g.

FREE BONUS: 14 DAYS VEGETARIAN MEAL PLAN

The only way to get the best out of this 14-days vegetarian diet meal plan is to follow it meticulously and diligently till the end. In the course of carrying out this meal plan, you will get to discover the absence of meat, fish and eggs in your meals. On the other hand, this meal plan will help you get started on your quest to being a vegetarian and maintaining a healthy lifestyle.

DAY 1	
Plan ahead:	Ultra Decadent Breakfast Potatoes
Wake up Drink:	Energizing Ginger Detox Tonic
Breakfast food:	Soothing Ginger Tea Drink
	Ultra Decadent Breakfast Potatoes
Mid-morning Snack:	Crunchy Apple Granola Crumble
Lunch:	Rich Red Lentil Curry
	Fluffy Deep Dish Pizza
Mid-afternoon Snack:	Scrumptious Baked Potatoes
	Warm Pomegranate Punch
Dinner:	Healthy Pumpkin Risotto
	Super Aubergines
	Inexpensive Bean and Spinach Enchiladas
Dessert:	Super Tea Spiced Poached Pears
Before Bedtime:	Ultimate Mulled Wine

DAY 2	
Plan ahead:	Convenient Scrambled Tofu Burritos
Wake up Drink:	Energizing Ginger Detox Tonic
Breakfast food:	Fragrant Spiced Coffee
	Convenient Scrambled Tofu Burritos
Mid-morning Snack:	Crunchy Apple Granola Crumble
Lunch:	Yummy Lentil Rice Soup
	Rich Cornbread
Mid-afternoon Snack:	Fabulous Glazed Carrots
	Pleasant Lemonade
Dinner:	Filling Three-Bean Chili

	Fantastic Butternut Squash & Vegetables
Dessert:	Warming Baked Apples
Before Bedtime:	Rich Truffle Hot Chocolate

DAY 3

Plan ahead:	Pillowy Sandwich Bread
	Spectacular Pumpkin Butter
Wake up Drink:	Energizing Ginger Detox Tonic
Breakfast food:	Soothing Ginger Tea Drink
	Pillowy Sandwich Bread with Spectacular Pumpkin Butter
Mid-morning Snack:	Crunchy Apple Granola Crumble
Lunch:	Incredible Artichoke and Olives Pizza
	Healthy Cabbage Soup
Mid-afternoon Snack:	Wonderful Glazed Root Vegetables
Dinner:	Bursting Black Bean Soup
	Tastiest Barbecued Tofu and Vegetables
Dessert:	Sumptuous Blueberry Lemon Cake
Before Bedtime:	Nice Spiced Cherry Cider

DAY 4

Plan ahead:	Scrumptious Spinach and Mushrooms Quiche
Wake up Drink:	Energizing Ginger Detox Tonic
Breakfast food:	Fragrant Spiced Coffee
	Scrumptious Spinach and Mushrooms Quiche
Mid-morning Snack:	Crunchy Apple Granola Crumble
Lunch:	Bursting Black Bean Soup
	Warm Spiced Lemon Drink
Mid-afternoon Snack:	Spicy Black-Eyed Peas
	Pleasant Lemonade
Dinner:	Mushroom and Peppers Pizza
	Exquisite Banana, Apple, and Coconut Curry
	Vibrant Minestrone
Dessert:	Heavenly Chocolate Peanut Butter Cake

Before Bedtime: Ultimate Mulled Wine

DAY 5	
Plan ahead:	Cozy Oatmeal with Cinnamon & Apple
Wake up Drink:	Energizing Ginger Detox Tonic
Breakfast food:	Soothing Ginger Tea Drink
	Cozy Oatmeal with Cinnamon & Apple
Mid-morning Snack:	Crunchy Apple Granola Crumble
Lunch:	Hearty Black Lentil Curry
Mid-afternoon Snack:	Fluffy Whole Wheat Potato Rolls
Dinner:	Creamy Creamed Corn
	Delightful Coconut Vegetarian Curry
Dessert:	Super Tea Spiced Poached Pears
Before Bedtime:	Rich Truffle Hot Chocolate

DAY 6	
Plan ahead:	Healthful Lentil and Rice Stew
Wake up Drink:	Energizing Ginger Detox Tonic
Breakfast food:	Fragrant Spiced Coffee
	Healthful Lentil and Rice Stew
Mid-morning Snack:	Crunchy Apple Granola Crumble
Lunch:	Remarkable Three-Grain Medley
	Tasty Tomato Garlic Mozzarella Pizza
Mid-afternoon Snack:	Scrumptious Baked Potatoes
	Warm Pomegranate Punch
Dinner:	Savory Spanish Rice
	Creamy Sweet Potato & Coconut Curry
Dessert:	Fudgy Chocolate Pudding Cake
Before Bedtime:	Nice Spiced Cherry Cider

DAY 7	
Plan ahead:	Mouthwatering Breakfast Quinoa
Wake up Drink:	Energizing Ginger Detox Tonic
Breakfast food:	Soothing Ginger Tea Drink
	Mouthwatering Breakfast Quinoa

Mid-morning Snack:	Crunchy Apple Granola Crumble
Lunch:	Tangy Barbecue Tofu Pizza
	Tangy Corn Chowder
Mid-afternoon Snack:	Spicy Black-Eyed Peas
Dinner:	Fuss-Free Cabbage and Tomatoes Stew
	Creamy Garlic Cauliflower Mashed Potatoes
Dessert:	Sumptuous Blueberry Lemon Cake
Before Bedtime:	Tangy Spiced Cranberry Drink

DAY 8

Plan ahead:	Chewy Olive Parmesan Bread
	Satisfying Wild Rice Breakfast Porridge
Wake up Drink:	Energizing Ginger Detox Tonic
Breakfast food:	Fragrant Spiced Coffee
	Chewy Olive Parmesan Bread
	Satisfying Wild Rice Breakfast Porridge
Mid-morning Snack:	Crunchy Apple Granola Crumble
Lunch:	Smoky Red Beans and Rice
	Chunky Pumpkin Spinach Chili
Mid-afternoon Snack:	Fluffy Whole Wheat Potato Rolls
	Warm Pomegranate Punch
Dinner:	Savory Squash & Apple Dish
	Chunky Pumpkin Spinach Chili
Dessert:	Heavenly Chocolate Peanut Butter Cake
Before Bedtime:	Nice Spiced Cherry Cider

DAY 9

Plan ahead:	Nutritious Chocolate & Cherry Oatmeal
Wake up Drink:	Energizing Ginger Detox Tonic
Breakfast food:	Soothing Ginger Tea Drink
	Nutritious Chocolate & Cherry Oatmeal
Mid-morning Snack:	Crunchy Apple Granola Crumble
Lunch:	Lovely Parsnip & Split Pea Soup
	Rich Cornbread
Mid-afternoon Snack:	Wonderful Glazed Root Vegetables
	Pleasant Lemonade

Dinner:	Rich Red Lentil Curry
	Flavorful Sweet Potatoes with Apples
	Wonderful Steamed Artichoke
Dessert:	Fudgy Chocolate Pudding Cake
Before Bedtime:	Ultimate Mulled Wine

DAY 10

Plan ahead:	Convenient Scrambled Tofu Burritos
Wake up Drink:	Energizing Ginger Detox Tonic
Breakfast food:	Fragrant Spiced Coffee
	Convenient Scrambled Tofu Burritos
Mid-morning Snack:	Crunchy Apple Granola Crumble
Lunch:	Exotic Butternut Squash and Chickpea Curry
Mid-afternoon Snack:	Fabulous Glazed Carrots
Dinner:	Sweet and Spicy Red Thai Vegetable Curry
	Healthy Coconut Basil Tofu
	Comforting Spinach and Artichoke Dip
Dessert:	Warming Baked Apples
Before Bedtime:	Rich Truffle Hot Chocolate

DAY 11

Plan ahead:	Nourishing Whole-Grain Porridge
Wake up Drink:	Energizing Ginger Detox Tonic
Breakfast food:	Soothing Ginger Tea Drink
	Nourishing Whole-Grain Porridge
Mid-morning Snack:	Crunchy Apple Granola Crumble
Lunch:	Flavorful Refried Beans
	Chunky Potato Soup
	Rich Cornbread
Mid-afternoon Snack:	Wonderful Glazed Root Vegetables
	Warm Spiced Lemon Drink
Dinner:	Hearty Vegetarian Lasagna Soup
	Amazing Brussels Sprouts
Dessert:	Sumptuous Blueberry Lemon Cake
Before Bedtime:	Tangy Spiced Cranberry Drink

DAY 12

Plan ahead:	Heavenly Chocolate Oatmeal
Wake up Drink:	Energizing Ginger Detox Tonic
Breakfast food:	Fragrant Spiced Coffee
	Heavenly Chocolate Oatmeal
Mid-morning Snack:	Crunchy Apple Granola Crumble
Lunch:	Chunky Black Lentil Veggie Soup
	Rich Cornbread
Mid-afternoon Snack:	Scrumptious Baked Potatoes
	Pleasant Lemonade
Dinner:	Sweet Potato Chili
	Vegetable Soup
	Spicy Cajun Boiled Peanuts
Dessert:	Heavenly Chocolate Peanut Butter Cake
Before Bedtime:	Tangy Spiced Cranberry Drink

DAY 13

Plan ahead:	Hearty Millet Stew
Wake up Drink:	Energizing Ginger Detox Tonic
Breakfast food:	Soothing Ginger Tea Drink
	Hearty Millet Stew
Mid-morning Snack:	Crunchy Apple Granola Crumble
Lunch:	Sizzling Vegetarian Fajitas
	Comforting Quinoa Chili
Mid-afternoon Snack:	Spicy Black-Eyed Peas
	Pleasant Lemonade
Dinner:	Super tasty Vegetarian Chili
	Flavorful Roasted Peppers
Dessert:	Super Tea Spiced Poached Pears
Before Bedtime:	Nice Spiced Cherry Cider

DAY 14

Plan ahead:	Crusty Rosemary Bread
	Healthful Lentil and Rice Stew
Wake up Drink:	Energizing Ginger Detox Tonic

Breakfast food:	Fragrant Spiced Coffee
	Crusty Rosemary Bread
	Healthful Lentil and Rice Stew
Mid-morning Snack:	Crunchy Apple Granola Crumble
Lunch:	Delicious Chipotle Red Lentil Pizza
	Incredible Tomato Basil Soup
Mid-afternoon Snack:	Fluffy Whole Wheat Potato Rolls
	Warm Spiced Lemon Drink
Dinner:	Awesome Spinach Artichoke Soup
	Comforting Chickpea Tagine
Dessert:	Warming Baked Apples
Before Bedtime:	Rich Truffle Hot Chocolate

CONCLUSION

Indeed, a vegetarian diet is the healthiest diet one could ever adapt to, owing to its amazing plethora of benefits which includes preservation of the environment, lower risks of cardio related diseases like heart attack, chronic diseases and weight loss. On the completion of this cookbook, not only will you be enlightened on the ins and outs of the vegetarian dieting life style, but also, you will get to be strongly acquainted with the various patterns of this amazing diet. In addition, this cook book will also help you grow your slow cooking skills which at the end will enable you to create your own slow cooker recipes and easily transform regular vegetarian recipes into slow cooking ones.

Bon Appetit!

Made in the USA
Lexington, KY
16 July 2019